Alligators
in the
Swamp

Alligators in the Swamp

Power, Ministry, and Leadership

George B. Thompson, Jr., editor

Contributors
Beverly Thompson, George B. Thompson, Jr.,
Harvey K. Newman, and Jim Watkins

Foreword by the Honorable Andrew Young
Illustrations by Victoria Thompson

The Pilgrim Press
Cleveland

To Melva Wilson Costen, Ph.D.

Teacher par excellence
Scholar and author
Elder of the church
Faculty colleague and friend

One whose spirit makes
hearts sing and who uses power
in the service of ministry

The Pilgrim Press,
700 Prospect Avenue, Cleveland, Ohio 44115-1100,
thepilgrimpress.com

10 09 08 07 06 05   5 4 3 2 1

Library of Congress Cataloging-in-Publication Data

Alligators in the swamp : power, ministry, and leadership / George B.
   Thompson, Jr., editor ; contributors, Beverly Thompson ... [et al.].
      p. cm.
   Includes bibliographical references (p.   ).
   ISBN 0-8298-1671-2 (paper : alk. paper)
   1. Pastoral theology. 2. Christian leadership. 3. Power (Christian
theology) I. Thompson, George B. (George Button), 1951- II.
Thompson, Beverly.

   BV4011.3.A45 2005
   253--dc22

                                   2005050337

Table of Contents

Foreword

By the Honorable Andrew Young

More than a half-century ago, a young man folded his arms over his knees as he sat down on the cool grass to gaze out across the mountains. It was early summer; the trees were dark green and the bushes and wild flowers danced on a fresh wind as he ran by them up the mountain trail. Glistening in the warm sun, huffing still from his exhilarating ascent far ahead of his colleagues, this young man paused to reflect upon the beauty spread out far in front of him. He paused—and could not help but wonder about his own life that lay ahead. Where was he going? What would God call him to do? How would he respond to the challenges with which a young African American male in the 1950s would be confronted, so starkly and sometimes violently?

In the years that followed, the young man graduated from seminary, got married, raised children, and did things that he never could have imagined that day on the mountain. America changed dramatically and deeply in those decades, and he became drawn into the center of many of those changes. His "career," if you could call it that, was as diverse as one could be—pastor, national religious staff person, civil rights activist, congressman, ambassador, urban mayor, entrepreneur with a global scope. If it had been possible to know the future, I am not sure if that young man on the mountain ever would have managed to develop the courage to face it all.

I know this because I was that young man. As I sought to allow God to guide me in my Christian calling, I had to learn how to overcome my own inner fears. Such fears were not unfounded, especially during the most intense days of the civil rights movement. Institutional racism is nothing to treat glibly, as all people of color in the United States intrinsically understand. Like many in my generation, I have stared squarely at power and wondered what to do. In those early years of my ministry, I grew more skilled in dealing with all forms of power. Persons like my first wife, Jean, and Dr. Martin Luther King, Jr., were instrumental in helping me develop both the internal and social resources that I needed. No one who is effective and beneficent with power learns "how" on their own.

I am pleased to commend this book as a resource for learning the ins and outs of power. This edited volume has grown out of a public ministry project in Atlanta to which I have given my enthusiastic support. It is called "Faith and the City," and it began in 1999 as an effort among three Atlanta seminaries (Candler School of Theology, Columbia Theological Seminary, and the Interdenominational Theological Center) to increase the religious voice once again in matters of the public good. The writers of these chapters have been very active in Faith and the City and present here a wide-ranging look at the phenomenon of power. Their purpose is not to argue for a particular biblical or theological view. Instead, they offer several different angles that show us power as it is. As I read through the chapters, I recognize many insights that I have learned the hard way, insights that are teachable and ultimately practical.

Religious communities in the twenty-first century face many complex challenges. Here in Atlanta, we continue to witness the world moving to our doorstep. Social values and practices are in flux, technology keeps making the world smaller and faster, creation itself is threatened, forms of violence have become daily news. How well-prepared are churches, synagogues, mosques, temples, and other religious communities to exercise power for the benefit of all God's world? What does it take for women and men called by God to religious vocations to acquire the perspectives, the skills, *and* the courage to actually lead God's people?

This volume opens up a conversation about power, faith, and leadership that has been a long time coming. Its authors draw upon resources from their own teaching disciplines as well as from their experiences as pastors. They seek to show how a multifaceted approach to power provides rich, in-depth ways to engage power faithfully and constructively. This book is more useful than a "how-to" manual. It explains concepts clearly and helps the reader see how these concepts can be put into practice. This allows the book to be adaptable to many, many kinds of situations that, at first glance, might not seem to have much in common.

Our nation's many churches exist with at least an implicit responsibility to share the good news beyond their own doors. Any effort to witness to the faith involves power. I encourage readers to keep this book close at hand, to reread and study as occasions demand. There are alligators in every swamp. Once you know how to handle the one inside of you, you are ready to help make your swamp a blessed place for all of its creatures.

Preface

Their new pastor arrived young, ambitious, energetic—and very naïve. It was one of those congregations that, in decades past, had commanded some air of prestige within its rural hamlet. Descendants of original settlers, although aging, held virtually all of the congregation's top elected positions. The town's recently retired mayor had joined the church three and one-half decades earlier. In spite of these connections, the town viewed this congregation as "cold and stuffy," its heritage tracing back farther than any of the other congregations tucked away along turns here and there in the tight valley.

The search committee had told him that they wanted to grow. "Attract young families with children" was specifically what they said. He could easily see the reason why: The congregation's 100 members were two-thirds over the age of sixty-five; Sunday school attendance was down to a trickle; the women worried that there was no one to which they could hand off their many duties and responsibilities. So our young pastor was ready to take this tottering congregation at its word. In a community that was steadily growing, his new church call was slowly dying.

Four and one-half years later, this young pastor accepted a call to a larger congregation across the country. He was older, tired of being frustrated, and not sure if he had learned anything. During his tenure, several young families either had begun attending or joined the church. Their children, along with neighboring kids from unchurched families, enjoyed day trips in the summer, vacation church school, weekly Sunday school, and a time of their own in worship. High school youth led liturgy; a few young parents were elected to the governing board; a contemporary songbook was added to the church pews, and a few of the older members died. While he had developed helpful pastoral relationships with several marginal families, he felt like the congregation as a whole was apathetic. A few times, committees approved his ideas and did nothing about them. Not even the weekly contacts that he had initiated with a few area pastors were enough to sustain him.

On his last Sunday, he shed a few tears as he said goodbye to those who had gathered for his final sermon. Yet he was not sad at all to be leaving. That church had seemed to him to have a mind of its own, dominated by a few old-timers who could not accept that change was coming. Hardly anyone in town appeared to care whether the congregation existed, and the church itself did almost nothing to reach beyond its own doors. If ever there was a good reason for an earnest and hard-working minister to leave a church, this young pastor certainly felt that he had one.

Five years later he was asking himself many of the same pastoral questions as before—only now they were becoming more focused. By this time, our pastor in question had worked for four congregations in eleven years. He had served in the capacities of assistant pastor, pastor, associate pastor, and interim pastor, in three states and three different time zones. In spite of the wide diversity of these pastoral settings, he was beginning to wonder more about what made them alike than what made them different.

The story of this young pastor's sojourns in ministry is one that I know well. It happens to be my own story, but—more significantly—I believe that it is a story that runs parallel to that of many other pastors. Too many of us spend too many years feeling too frustrated and too discouraged. As a result, we end up getting seriously ill, our family life suffers, some of us drop out of pastoral ministry—and some of us even question the validity of our own calling. And what about the congregations that we sought to serve faithfully? Is there something wrong with them, that they should end pastoral relationships on such sour notes? Surely these sad partings don't happen only in the small congregations, who already have so much going against them in a society that worships size and glitz. What happens to churches in the long run, when their pastors leave so unhappy?

These are serious questions that need the sustained attention of denominations and seminaries alike. They are questions that more and more of us seek to answer. Ministry in the twenty-first century promises to become even more complex. The challenges already boggle the minds of faithful pastors and church members. To complicate matters, our market-oriented American society encourages a fad approach to seeking solutions for our needs. What resources truly will help? What perspectives, and which tools, hold the greatest promise for assisting pastors in leading congregations through faithful Gospel witness?

This book seeks to answer these questions indirectly, by exploring a topic that churches and pastors tend to neglect. That topic is power—not a "pie-in-the-sky, by and by" version of power, but a day-to-day, dead-serious, in-your-face version. Rather than retreating to idealistic, theological language, this book aims its sights on the actual practice of power in human life. This kind of power can be—and has been—studied and described by scholars without a particular theological axe to grind. This kind of power operates in, around, and beyond every human being every single day. This kind of power often hurts our churches and their pastors because no one is willing to admit that it is present.

What my colleagues and I seek to do in this book, then, is to help the church of the future by naming power for what it is. Theological affirmations of power serve little value unless they acknowledge in concrete ways the reality of power in human affairs. Why else do biblical prophets like Isaiah and Jeremiah spend so much time speaking God's word to specific communities and nations in very specific situations? Power affects all of us; it influences and exists in our congregations; it can be both beneficent and malevolent in its purpose. Churches and pastors need to understand power more clearly if they are to be prepared for the coming world— one like none ever seen before.

Because this is a book for pastors and the churches that they serve, its focus will not be historical or purely theoretical. Instead, the authors in this book seek to show how our various approaches to power actually can help pastors and churches do ministry. Accomplishing this goal requires that we blend theory with issues of practice. This is not easy work, so we expect that the reader will experience some "work" in the reading. If something as fundamental as power is not well-understood in our churches, then surely it is not unreasonable for us to devote substantial time and energy to learning about it. Otherwise, all of our efforts to strengthen spiritual communities could become unwittingly undermined.

A discussion like the one being undertaken here easily could take on a somber, antagonistic, and even fatalistic tone. This would be unfortunate and not very productive. Because we believe that God has a sense of humor, we decided to frame our discussion of power with a particular metaphor. The images of alligators and swamps help us tell the story that we think needs to be told about power in a way that our chuckling will instruct us. We will say more about this metaphor in chapter one. It is enough for now to point out that swamps and alligators are part of God's creation, so they play their roles in God's purposes. So, also, does power. Perhaps the only way that we can learn to deal with power for the good of the gospel is to have a sense of humor about it.

The origins of this book must be credited to the stimulus of "Faith and the City" (FATC). This unique venture has brought together theological schools in metro Atlanta, to strengthen and expand public religious leadership. The Interdenominational Theological Center (ITC), Columbia Theological Seminary, and Candler School of Theology have been involved since 1999 in offering courses, certificates, special programs, student retreats, and the like for students, faculty, clergy, and interested laity and citizens. McAfee School of Theology joined the project in 2003. Through the skill and energy of the "downtown office," FATC reaches a wider public with a newsletter, an e-letter, an award-winning Web site (*www.faithandthecity.org*) and organizational initiatives and relationships. Momentum for this multiyear project stemmed from conversations among and commitments from the Hon. James Laney, the Hon. Andrew Young, and Dr. Robert Franklin. Support from Mr. Charles "Pete" McTier, president of the Community Foundation of Atlanta, has been articulate and essential.

While this volume is not an official FATC project, it has the fingerprints of Faith and the City all over it. Jim Watkins served for three years as Columbia's FATC director. Harvey Newman took Jim's place when he moved to South Carolina, and I have been part of FATC since its early days. Much of this material has been "field-tested" in presentations to a joint course, "Power, Faith, and Civic Leadership," in which students from ITC, Columbia, and Georgia State University all enroll. That course provided us with the conviction that this book will be useful to pastors, congregations, judicatories, and anyone of faith who seeks to contribute to the common good.

As editor, I am grateful for the camaraderie and commitment that spurred us authors along. Each one of us has something particular to say, something that offers insights on power and the church that are fresh and applicable. Years ago, a counselor and friend advised me, "Write about what you know." In the light of such advice, this book was written out of a great and useful store of knowledge. It was a new kind of joy for me to work with all of these colleagues. It was a new experience also to write with Beverly, my wife, herself a seasoned pastor and very skilled counselor and spiritual director. Perhaps it was most rewarding, however, to collaborate on the line-drawing illustrations with my daughter Victoria. She and her generation should be enough reason for the subject of this book.

Alligators and Swamps: Power and the World of Parish Ministry

by George B. Thompson, Jr.

1

Vignettes

When I was in first grade, I could hit a softball over the heads of the outfielders. One corner of the playground was used as a ball diamond for "the little kids," since the real baseball field was larger and farther back from the school building. So we little kids gathered at our appointed spot, boys and girls alike, dividing quickly into makeshift teams, to celebrate America's great pastime. During those recess breaks, I must have hit enough home runs through and around the least-experienced players (after all, don't coaches always stick the worst players in summer league in the outfield?) to have imagined myself good. I can still hear myself rounding the bases, boasting, "I'm the Mickey Mantle of the first grade!" It is one of my earliest memories of exhilaration.

Such moments, as the years went by, turned out to be few and far between. By the time that all of my brothers and I reached grade school, we had begun practicing on each other the verbal art of "one-up." It seemed as though I never could win—which felt somewhat ignominious, since I assumed that this coveted position naturally would fall to the oldest, even if it were only by eleven minutes. Yet, both my twin brother and I found ourselves more often than we would care to admit stymied by the oral sparring of our other two brothers. Winning arguments had a way of being recognized immediately by all. The only thing worse to me was the visual display upon the victor's face, that look of sly exultation. I suppose that I reached a point in adolescence when I decided that it was beneath me to risk such defeat at their hands.

Years before I deigned to stoop to this almost-certain trouncing, though, my brothers and I were learning how to use our hands, not just our mouths. Summertime was not filled with "lazy, hazy days" for us, but rather with early and long days of field work. For ten weeks of the summer, we boarded a faded, old school bus at 6 A.M. and rode for an hour to a strawberry field (June) or a pole bean field (July and August). There, we picked the crop of the season for seven to eight hours, with about a half-hour break for lunch. We did not think the work particularly difficult, but it was tedious, calling forth creative ways to fill the time without incurring discipline from the adult supervisors ("row bosses") who patrolled the fields. As I got older, my goal was to pick enough strawberries or beans in one day to be the "winner" that day. Prizes were modest, but recognition made up for that. Becoming the season winner was something that I gave up pursuing, since I knew who the hardest, fastest pickers were. So I hoped for a day when they were sick at home or got assigned to a series of poorly-yielding rows.

My ten seasons of field labor did lead to a significant pay-off in the long run. My best season in either beans or berries led to a check for $108 and change. I felt rich! But I knew, as always, that this money was not for spending; it went into the savings account that my parents helped me to set up when I was nine years old. Eight years later, that account had more than enough money in it for me to pay my way on a month-long study tour of Europe. For a small-town boy, it was the trip of a lifetime. Somehow, I sensed that many of the other teens who went on this trip did not pay for it themselves. Knowing that I had used my own earned funds gave me my first big experience of what money could do.

It was also during my teenage years that I experienced what probably was my only undefeated streak in any venture. For six years, I won every student body election for which I ran. It began with being chosen by my peers to be student council representative for my homeroom. That streak ran for four semesters straight, until I was elected to a school-wide office for the third year. Once in high school, my success continued. After another year as homeroom representative, I was elected to school-wide offices two years in a row. I learned a lot of parliamentary procedure along the way—a valuable resource after I was ordained. I attended meetings of Rotary, city council, and other community organizations. I represented my home state in a national student convention held all the way across the continent. Although I always felt nervous during elections, I nonetheless had reached a point where I believed deep down that this was "my" place. I was the best person for the job, I thought, and the electorate should respond accordingly.

What do stories of first-grade softball, sibling arguments, picking strawberries, and student government have in common? As I look back, I can see in all of them my earliest experiences with power. I felt some sense of enviable accomplishment as a very young, aspiring athlete. I went through the common childhood occurrence of being thwarted as I sought a certain momentary supremacy among my brothers. I learned the potential in saving money as a means to deferred yet desirable goals. I encountered for several years both the privilege and responsibility that accrue with elected office. Each one of these vignettes represents a form of power that is widely understood. Certainly in the middle of any of those moments, I would not have been capable of articulating much of anything about power in theoretical terms. The fact that such conversations are difficult to undertake—even at adult, erudite levels—suggests one reason for this book. Power is something that every one of us experiences, in many and quite varied ways. Our understanding of power can be accurate for any particular context or set of circumstances, even while it rarely can be comprehensive.

Compare, by way of illustration, my childhood memories with images such as police cars, courtrooms, the New York Stock Exchange, state capitol buildings, voting booths, an anti-war rally, and the like. If as a teenager entering college, I had articulated "everything I knew about power," how well would I have expressed the wider realities of the American democratic government and a capitalist economy? My early experiences provided starting points for learning to understand complex dynamics today that create, grant, and limit power. They are just that—starting points. All the proverbial wisdom in the world still does not manage to capture the breadth and complexity of something that all of us know exists but cannot fully explain.

I don't think I have this
"alligator" thing figured out yet.

Why This Book

These comments apply just as much to the actual lived experience of churches as it does to any other human community. Most people would acknowledge that the existence and activity of power in human experience is real. When, then, is power so difficult to accept within a community of believers? In my experience as a pastor and teacher in the church, I have been struck by how power is recognized so ambiguously and ambivalently. It is not so much that congregations fail to affirm the sovereignty and purposes of God in their lives of worship and witness. At one level, this kind of affirmation seems often to be so unquestioningly accepted that its very strength becomes dulled. Rather, what arrests my attention time and again is the unwillingness in church bodies to treat human dimensions of power as one of the divine resources for responsible stewardship.

This book was conceived out of the conviction that "power in the church" is a barely understood and thus potentially abused notion. In our efforts to be authentically faithful believers, we Christians tend to play down the human side of the Gospel message, namely, that God was in Christ, reconciling the world to God's self (2 Corinthians 5:18–19). It seems that the Incarnation too often is so framed to suggest that God had to jump into the mess of humanity just long enough to straighten it out and then get out. After the Resurrection and Ascension, this line of thought goes, the Godhead can return to divine bliss, since the purposes of God negate the value of creation. What does this spin on the doctrine of Incarnation do to our human encounters with human power? It leaves us struggling with a view of God's power as holy and good and human power as inherently evil. If we do not believe in our bones that God's creation is redeemable, we will have a hard time reconciling the power that is in our human midst.

Some Claims about Power

I write, then, guided by several basic claims about power. These assertions seem to me to be worth highlighting, if church bodies are to pursue their vocations with wisdom and blessed consequence. These are claims that will not be defended explicitly but will depend upon the cogency of the book as a whole to be persuasive. One of these is simply that *power exists*. In human reality, power is what it is. Power exists, because we could not survive or function—individually as well as collectively—without the ability to accomplish things. Yet it is evident that "the ability to accomplish" sometimes is exercised against the will of other persons or groups. In such scenarios, we become aware of potential problems. At the least, human communities certainly do identify circumstances in which power has been used for improper ends. Crimes, for instance, fit this version of power.

Acknowledging the risk of power's abuse, however, leads us toward the problem of the baby and the bathwater. Do you throw both of them out? Of course not. The fact that power can be and does get abused does not mean that power in and of itself is bad or

When it comes to power, everyone wants a piece of the action.

wrong. This assertion undergirds our second claim: that *power is inherently neutral.* This claim might not be supported by every theologian in a historical theology course, which is one reason why it needs to be highlighted here. We get ourselves into awkward and sometimes downright contradictory situations if we seek to demonize power in itself.

Having asserted these first two claims, we are led to realize also that *power is easier to recognize than it is to define.* As we will see later in this chapter, universal definitions of power are very difficult to develop and even harder to agree to. This book, therefore, does not spend much time defining power as one thing or another, without any wiggle room for clarification remaining. Instead, the book looks at power as it can be viewed in four distinct ways. We will say more about this toward the end of this chapter.

Because our vantage point for this book is congregations and pastors, these three basic claims suggest a fourth one. It is fundamental to the implicit argument of this book to accept the view that *power can be better understood and utilized only by integrating theological thinking with descriptive, empirical disciplines.* This claim might appear more complicated than the others, yet its purpose is straightforward. Church people must learn to think about power not only with the idealistic language of their faith, but also by using language from those branches of learning that seek to understand things as they are. Let us spend a little more time laying out this point.

Language from church—language that expresses our religious conviction, our awareness of God, and God's leading in and purposes for life—is one kind of discourse. It speaks in terms that cannot be verified easily (if at all!) outside of the commitment of those who accept a path of divine faith. For centuries, this kind of language dominated Western thought, incorporating the other established academic disciplines into a fairly uniform worldview and educational process.[1] Over time, however, various new influences spread, leading to the development of intellectual inquiry focused upon hard evidence observable in the natural world. This new form of science was "modern" since it was based upon conclusions derived from the data, rather than from a theological position. Students of modern history easily recognize the secularizing effect of this science: It tended to drive a wedge between truth that could be proven and truth that had to be accepted "on faith." [2]

This dichotomy between faith and reason, I believe, has had a negative effect upon our common Christian perspective on power. This common view assumes that in this perspective the only legitimate power comes from God—which then means that it is not subject to the same kind of scrutiny as other phenomena (e.g., biological and chemical processes, geologic features, weather, etc.). Sincere persons of faith therefore conclude that, if only divine power can be good, all other expressions of power are bad. Such a conclusion (often formed at the unconscious level—see chapter three) leads finally to what I see to be all sorts of practical problems. What do we make of our own abilities to accomplish things? How do we distinguish between the divine and sinful uses of power in, say, a church governing board? Why should Christian citizens submit to laws in society?

The alternative to this stalemate over Christian views on power is to approach the matter with an inclusive, rather than exclusive, method. That is, as the claim states above, believers should examine power *both* in terms of originating in God *and* in terms of human capacity. Because so many research fields now study human beings and their behavior, we in the religious sphere have these partners available, whose resources provide significant analysis and insight. An inclusive method as encouraged here promises to make our understandings of power more accurate, more nuanced, and ultimately more useful.

It probably should be said here also that engaging an inclusive method for understanding power does not come readily. Our Western way of thinking prefers to separate and distinguish between apparent opposites as though they mutually exclude each other. You might discover that some of your own confusion is based upon being unfamiliar with "both/and" thinking—that is, inclusive and holistic. You certainly will discover this confusion among colleagues and friends. That should not stop you from looking for the bigger picture, seeking to see power in all of its richness.

A fifth claim considers power's location. This point needs to be stated early, since much study of leadership tends to focus upon traits of individual persons. Rather than assuming that power resides only in certain individuals, I submit that *power needs to be understood in terms both of individual and of community.* This statement might appear to be unnecessary until we consider how American society has become heavily individualistic. The dominant stream in the United States emphasizes the existence and rights of the person almost to the exclusion of community. Power then is perceived as residing within particular persons. In the view of this book, power exists much more broadly than solely within individuals. Power occurs in relationships—not just personal relationships, but between a person and a group, between groups, between clusters of groups, and so on. Power is not within the reach merely of certain persons but plays out in a myriad of human connections and situations. Accepting this claim helps us avoid oversimplifying analysis of power—a dangerous thing to do, especially in churches.

One final claim will help us set the stage for the discussion that follows. It can be stated in practical terms: *Most church people—lay and clergy alike—confuse power with authority.* What is the difference, and why does it matter? Think for a moment about a candidate elected to city council. Supporters cheer for her and wave signs. The candidate beams with pleasure and makes earnest promises about what is going to happen as a result of her election. Consider at the same time the pastor whose bishop has appointed him to a new parish charge. Do either of these persons have any power on their first day at the job? The answer is not nearly what they think! Both a public official and a pastor hold an office, which is granted certain authority by virtue of the respective governing bodies. That authority includes rights and responsibilities of action, some of which the officeholder (pastor or elected official) might be able to exercise without resistance. However, most of us who have held any kind of office learn rather quickly that most of the power develops over time, as the officeholder develops trust, respect, and persuasiveness. I have discussed this distinction for pastors in another book, arguing for the necessity of the pastor being "adopted" by the congregation.[3] Yes, there certainly is power involved among pastor and congregation, but no, it is not granted automatically through office.

Power-Related Church Literature

The influence of theories and definitions sometimes can be difficult to trace in religious thought. At the level of popular church literature, analyses and critiques take a back seat to practical applications. Still, power is a topic that we find laced throughout much of the recent literature of the last twenty-five years or so. It is not always easy to spot, however, since power usually has been discussed in the context of other subjects—such as church conflict. Conflict in many ways is a more concrete theme, and for years in congregations and denominations it has been on a continuous rise. The Alban Institute's Speed Leas devoted much of his consulting ministry to developing tools for congregational conflict management.[4]

In the 1990s, more books on congregational conflict began to appear.[5] These publications generally follow the Leas goal of resolution, so they concentrate on learning how to resolve the disagreement. Conflict here is seen as an accelerated set of circumstances that has become at least partially public within the congregation. As the circumstances intensify, two similar groups in the church emerge and oppose the other's position, while a larger third group often remains noncommittal but confused and troubled. Certainly power is at stake for all parties. Since these books offer a process toward resolution, however, they give scant attention to power as it is. As is often the case with publications for church audiences, the content is long on "how to *do* it" and short on "how do we first *frame* it?"

Let us look a little more closely at a few other earlier resources that help to set the stage for why a book like this one is necessary.

Power and Stress

Perhaps the most interesting of the earliest current works to touch on power and church is John Harris's *Stress, Power and Ministry.* Subtitled "An Approach to the Current Dilemmas of Pastors and Congregations," Harris writes in recognition of the ongoing social and demographic upheavals underway in many American communities. He understands the pivotal role that the pastor plays in helping congregations to change in response to contextual change.[6] He insightfully points out the necessity for the congregation to embrace, rather than expel, stresses and the pastor's delicate but significant part in that embrace.[7] He asserts that power occurs among people in the course of their life together, optimally on the basis of shared esteem.[8] He spells out four ways that influence can operate between pastor and congregation.[9] Throughout the book, he discusses the paralyzing effects of fear and the crucial role of the pastor in helping the congregation deal with anxiety constructively.[10]

However, Harris's exploration of stress and power in ministry spends no time exploring the nature of the upheavals themselves that churches continue to face today. This style of generalized reference to external conditions is typical of books designed for clergy and congregations. My reason for making this point here is to suggest that it indicates the difficulty of understanding power adequately. In Harris's book, this critique is most evident through his definition of power, in which he follows a psychological model from Rollo May. Power in this frame has to do with being able to bring about something different in someone else. Yet, almost in the same breath, Harris speaks of institutional and operational factors as two of the three with which pastors struggle. Even the third one, personal, is not private, since it deals with "confusion about [pastors'] own roles in the parish."[11] In other words, all of the references to parish, community, and society are treated in terms of the role of the pastor and what is needed from the person who fills that role.

Thus, in spite of his many insights that apply yet today, Harris's discussion of power remains primarily defined by psychological and interpersonal categories.[12] In retrospect, this psychological parameter limits Harris's contribution. Sources, types, and occasions for power beyond the person are not treated. Power in its complex fullness remains to be explicated, using wider models. Harris's book still warrants study by ministry practitioners because it opens up a conversation that today can engage other disciplines as well.

Analyzing Power
Roy Oswald's short work, *Power Analysis of A Congregation,*[13] is one of the few in religious literature to discuss power directly. Here, Oswald first speaks anecdotally and theologically about his maturing

understanding of power. He believes that power is not by nature either benevolent or malevolent, but that all power has a divine source.[14] Furthermore, power to Oswald is not a limited commodity. It can and should be allowed to flourish within a community in order to benefit everyone.[15] Drawing from secular sources, Oswald sketches out a model of power. Power operates personally in four possible ways, corporately in three possible ways, and within the links between a person and the congregation.[16] Using this model, Oswald says, can help a person figure out the power dynamics of any specific (especially tense) situation.

Oswald's model provides church people with a practical analytical tool that is not too complicated. Since it focuses on analysis itself, the model helps church folks to step back from a situation to assess it first. Many pastors would benefit from a "look before you leap" strategy like this one! Since the model also combines both individual and group dimensions, it steers readers away from the common mistake of treating power only in individual terms. As we will see in the following chapters, power is most adequately understood in a comprehensive framework, one that seeks to account for its range of expressions.

Sadly, in my years as a pastor and seminary teacher, I can recall Oswald's model being mentioned by church folks only once. As useful as it could be, it appears to have languished amidst the burgeoning list of resources for congregations. This is unfortunate because many growing church conflicts would be channeled more productively by seriously engaging a tool like Oswald's.

"The Powers"
In any representative bibliography on church and power stands one particular work of singular value: Walter Wink's trilogy on "the powers," an exhaustive analysis and interpretation of power language in the New Testament and related literature. This work is, however, no abstract academic exercise. Wink's driving motivation for the study emerged from a sabbatical spent in Latin America. For two decades, he had been reflecting on the New Testament's affirmation of Christ's sovereignty over evil. The Latin American experience overwhelmed him with atrocious evidence of human-enacted

evil. Wink faced both a scholarly and a spiritual crisis, which worked its way through this research.[17]

What Wink concluded from his massive, unprecedented research study has provided a fascinating and challenging perspective on power. It required his use of several ancient and modern languages in order to search for the meaning of terms in the New Testament that are poorly understood. His work, then, is based in the discipline of biblical studies, but in his interpretation of the results, Wink implicitly draws from both philosophy and Jungian psychology. In so doing, Wink nonetheless seeks to avoid reducing "the powers" to modern categories that explain them away.[18] Wink asserts that New Testament power has a spiritual dimension that cannot be ignored.[19] Yet he also asserts that the modern Western worldview has led to inaccurate treatment of the nature of this spiritual power.[20]

As an alternative, Wink submits that the spiritual quality of power cannot be separated from its physical demonstration. Spiritual power, he claims, is "the innermost essence" of physical/material power, so that "the powers are simultaneously the outer and inner aspects of one and the same indivisible concretion of power."[21] Here is where philosophy comes into play in Wink's work: He believes that viewing New Testament powers in this way requires a shift to "a unitary worldview," distinct from the scientific worldview that has dominated modernity.[22]

This naming of power leads Wink to identify spirit as something that exists within human communities. He argues that all human institutions take on a life of their own, "a suprahuman quality" that pervades all aspects of behavior and thought. Institutional existence becomes self-perpetuating in the most subtle ways, guided by the spiritual power that is created within it.[23]

Wink's theses must be understood as an attempt to shift our paradigm of understanding about power. They are too rich to elaborate and critique here. For our purposes, it is useful to the course of this book to acknowledge three points. One is to recognize that this major study has been done, that such an extensive scrutiny and interpretation of a major religious document offers considerably provocative insights about power. A second point is that one of the disciplines available for Christians in seeking to understand power is biblical studies. This point should not surprise anyone: the church affirms the centrality of the Scriptures in its faith, life, and witness. The third point, however, might seem less evident. It is that the journey to comprehending power almost inevitably will take us along paths that seem unfamiliar or even inappropriate. Wink's study, driven as it was by the need to reconcile doctrine with reality, forced him to look beyond conventional methods of interpreting his data. As he framed his views on the New Testament witness, he had to say things in a new way. This is a common, but potentially frightening, experience whenever we aim to make sense out of something that old explanations seem frail to support. Similarly, some readers of this book will feel a certain uneasiness at points with what they discover here.

Conflict in the New Testament

A different kind of analytical methodology with biblical material is evident in Dudley and Hilgert's study of the earliest Christian communities.[24] These two authors are particularly interested in seeing how community stress and conflict were understood and played out in the New Testament. To address this question, they use historical biblical criticism and the social sciences together, a rather novel (but not unique) approach.[25] Their topics include how these earliest communities were formed, how they struggled between being sectarian and being accepted, and how they dealt with conflict. The term "power" is not used in any central way, although any discussion of church tensions inevitably deals with power. The absence of a direct treatment makes this book less useful for our purposes, as do its very brief references to lessons for church life today. Yet for those who appreciate biblical study and are ready to learn something new, the book offers a substantial background for seeing "things as they are"—for churches today.

As samples of available literature, the books mentioned in this section represent the general state of discussion about church and power fairly accurately. Oswald and Dudley/Hilgert demonstrate, perhaps more clearly than any of the others, the value of applying descriptive disciplines such as anthropology and political science to church life. What makes the present volume distinctive, then, is its analytical attention to human power as a central topic to religious life. As a subject worthy of study, then, the phenomena of power have changed over many centuries in their structures and processes. What first world citizens experience today of power has its roots in a past that is mostly unfamiliar. Yet that past can serve to indicate why power deserves attention, even from American churches today.

Hey, Little feller—It's my way or the highway!

History and Context

Without a historical view of any subject, our grasp of it will be partial, incomplete, and thus misleading. It is instructive, then, for us to look back and identify far-reaching movements and changes in history that gave rise to the world as we now experience it. That world, dominated for centuries as it had been by Western European life and practice, did not always allow much free rein for human power. A review of the most basic features of the Middle Ages reminds us that human structures were much more limited in scale and complexity than they are now. In other words, the specific dynamics of power in medieval Europe resulted directly from the ways in which human communities were allowed to be organized.

Historical Shifts in Power

Two categories that most directly affect these structures and their changes are politics and economics. After the decline and eventual dissolution of the Roman Empire through the fifth century c.e., the European continent was divided into several kingdoms.[26] Politically, the centralized authority from Rome gave way to a more feudalistic system, where local lords sought control over particular lands, currying favor with a monarch. Even Charlemagne's ninth-century effort to restore the Roman Empire did not succeed in unifying much land or many ruling structures.[27] Politically, most communities remained rural and subservient; economically, they subsisted. Power was concentrated in the hands of the few who managed to take control over certain territory and maintain it through a feudal compact.[28] Feudal authority could be tenuous, and it meant, as throughout most of history, that the vast majority of people had no influence on things beyond their immediate daily circumstances.

As centuries went by, these political and economic structures and practices gradually changed, laying the foundations for life in the West as we know it today. These changes rarely were received without resistance by monarchs and church officials, who realized that they would be losing not simply official authority, but the actual capacity to get what they wanted—power itself. As feudalism gave way to nation-creating in the late Middle Ages, a new form of economy gradually emerged. Italians who had become wealthy from Asian trade markets began to reinvest their profits into ventures. Business people in other European countries followed suit, creating their own economic empires in various regions and segments of trade. Partnerships, often within one family, were established to develop companies for commerce, displacing the traditional medieval guild. Merchants found ways of doing business with early forms of credit; banks widened their extension of charging interest (as the church gradually eased its opposition to the practice). Certain families became famous and highly influential in this period, having made fortunes in commerce or banking.

As is the case with any major shift in history, these economic changes led to significant changes in both politics and society.[29] For one thing, the manorial way of life that had dominated medieval Europe was undermined. Towns were founded again, developing as centers of exchange for villages in their regions. Money, rather than exchanges of goods or services, was used increasingly for payment. This meant that the major indicators of wealth were shifting from land to portable assets, such as cash, goods, and maritime vessels. Peasants, whose livelihood depended upon the very localized, rural, agricultural setup of the manor, gradually developed economic options beyond the subsisting confines of field and village. A middle class, between that of the peasants and the nobility, grew by offering new skills to those with wealth and interest. Land was no longer controlled only by the nobles but could be purchased by merchants with their profits. Traditional official church opposition to material gain eroded as values of hard work, thrift, creativity, and risk blossomed in the changing European society. Status no longer was limited to hereditary rank; a person or family could become very prestigious through great success in business.

This very concise summary of developments in European political and economic structures forms the background for the establishment, first, of the English colonies in North America in the seventeenth century and, second, of the United States of America in the late-eighteenth century. The ability of one group of people to seek independence from another group is closely tied up with conditions that take time to develop or change. Forms of power that were possible in medieval times either had disappeared or were vastly adapted to new structures of national governance and economic activity. As we recall from high school social studies class, the democratic government that was created in the United States has spurred movements for the same in other nations. Indeed, one element of American political rhetoric yet today concerns the extent to which the United States has a right or responsibility to promote not only democracy but also capitalism around the world.

Development of democracy has contributed to changing forms of power even within society's economic realm. The power of land decreased in importance from medieval life into the early-modern period, while the structures of capitalism themselves underwent further change. Economist John Kenneth Galbraith points out that power has shifted away from the personal sway of flamboyant nineteenth-century entrepreneurs to the "faceless" style of corporate management.[30] As we will see shortly, this point extrapolates on a theme in the work of sociologist Talcott Parsons as well. Not only does power circulate between parties and entities; over time it can change its location and direction.

What does all this talk of history, politics, and economics have to do with power? Plenty. As I stated at the beginning of this section, the world in which we live came from somewhere. The problems that pastors face with their churches, and that churches face within themselves and their communities, occur on the stage of the kinds of power that the backdrops of democracy and capitalism have painted. We tend to take our beliefs about most things, including power, for granted. Those of you who have traveled and/or lived in Asia, Africa, or Latin America know from experience that Americans cannot take for granted their way of life. The "freedom of association" and the "mediating structures" that make possible much of the liberty and opportunity that Americans enjoy, grew out of a long and specific history.[31] True wisdom about the existence and nature of power today begins with awareness of the context within which it operates. This statement is no less true in the religious arena than it is for anything else.

Locating this Discussion Theoretically

As is always the case, religious treatment of a topic such as power can be located within a wider and longstanding intellectual conversation, one that heavily influences the religious version. Power has been a discussion in philosophy since antiquity even though many of us equate contemporary discussions exclusively with the academic discipline of political science. It would be impossible to summarize here either of these discussions adequately. What is feasible for our purposes is to demonstrate in general terms some major elements of those traditions that orient us to the approaches that follow in this book. Because our present goal is to speak to today's world, this summary treats power from sources out of the last century.[32]

One famous philosopher claims that his definition of power is measurable. Bertrand Russell defines power as "the production of intended effects." These effects in the human realm occur both with persons and with groups. He notes distinctions in types of power based on law, tradition, hereditary, "naked (i.e., with arms)," revolution, learning, and so on. Politics and government also express forms of power, both overtly and covertly.[33] Russell's categories are familiar enough, but his concise definition still leaves arguable questions about outcome, potential, and purpose. For instance, does someone have to aim for a particular outcome in order for it to be considered an act of power? Questions like these are not easily answered.

Max Weber, the famous social scientist of the early twentieth century, was particularly interested in power manifested in the economic realm of human life. The English translation of his term for this form of power is "domination," which affects social configurations as well. Weber's definition of domination as power has been used and critiqued widely:[34] it is "the possibility of imposing one's own will upon the behavior of other persons," a phenomenon that "can emerge in the most diverse forms."[35] (This definition, by the way, perhaps is the one that most of us would recognize easily.[36]) In his study of history, Weber sees domination occurring in the economic arrangements of feudal Europe as well as in modern market capitalism. In feudalism, this kind of control derives from the ability of one person (the lord) to command by right and expect obedience;

in capitalism, control derives from the interplay between those with available products and skills and others who desire those products and skills. Weber seeks to clarify that this use of the concept of domination is limited to rulers who can command obedience from subjects, that is, "authoritarian power of command."[37] His broader understanding of power emphasizes the feature of potential resistance by the other as well as the feature of unspecified traits that make possible the imposition of will.[38]

Much theorizing about power, then, focuses upon its political dimensions, as Robert Dahl puts it, "the identification of elites and leadership, the discovery of ways in which power is allocated to different strata, relations among leaders and between leaders and non-leaders, and so forth." One of Dahl's contributions to the discussion of power is to classify it into a number of categories, based upon observed data rather than generalized conceptualization, as in Russell's scheme.[39] Talcott Parsons pursues a similar end empirically but with the broader purpose of understanding society in general. Parsons criticizes what he sees to be an inadequate degree of analysis. He contends that political theory about power must be consistent within a broader design of social investigation, within which political theory finds its place.[40] Those who have studied Parsons know how technical and organized his treatment is of his subjects. His definition of power, predictably, is expressed in technical language that moves beyond the task of this book. However, his shorthand definition highlights an element that other theories do not necessarily emphasize: Parsons speaks of power in a society as "a circulating medium ["analogous to money"] moving back and forth over the boundaries of the polity."[41] The term "circulation" suggests how power can and does move around; it does not remain in one place or with one single source. Similar to Weber and many other theorists, Parsons recognizes this circulation especially between political and economic entities.[42] French philosopher Michel Foucault generalizes the same point: "Power must be analyzed as something which circulates,...It is never localized here or there,...Power is employed and exercised through a net-like organization."[43]

Other modern theorists of power have criticized both Weber and Parsons from the vantage point of Marxist thought. Following Marx's basic framework of analysis, scholar Nicos Poulantzas defines power in terms of class, a concept with references to society, economics, and politics. For Marxists, society cannot be understood adequately without acknowledging that its various classes conflict with each other over their particular class concerns. One class in a society will dominate others, thereby establishing a power relationship. Power, then, is defined in terms of class interests, namely, "the capacity of a social class to realize its specific objective interests."[44] A Marxist view of society and power treats individual persons in the context of society, not the other way around.

This quick review of modern theories of power reminds us that thoughtful persons have been thinking about power long and hard. As noted earlier, power is easy to see but not so easy to explain. Among these several scholarly claims rest a number of views and insights that should make sense to us in the church. Insights such as these should help to demonstrate to the church the value of thinking about power with resources that do not derive directly or solely from religion.

Method of This Book

Through this book, we will become keenly aware that power is always contextual. In the American setting, free-market capitalism (economic power) and representative democracy (political power) frame many of the ways that people live and interact. They make possible many— if not most—of our capacities for power. This is a point that some readers might find unnecessary to emphasize, preferring rather to plunge into a list of anecdotal advice about exercising power. We propose instead that recognizing our own context aids us in seeing power as it is, warts and all. Our method is not to begin with anecdotes or even religious ideals. In their place, we start with description by drawing upon analyses of power from four distinct (but, as you will see, related) vantage points. Our suggestions for religious practice derive from the conviction that religious people are theologically shaped, indeed—but, after all, they are human beings, too.

Such an approach might seem to some religious readers as false, misguided, or even heretical. These reservations have been addressed earlier in the chapter. All of the writers in this book are seminary-trained, ordained clergy with parish experience. In our efforts to do ministry in today's world, each one of us has discovered "nonreligious" resources that help to enlighten our understanding of engaging human life. There is danger if religious folks ignore serious, disciplined, secular study of life. We in the church trivialize power when we think of it only in theological terms. As I have suggested already, it seems like an insult to God to treat the created world as though it gives up no clues to its Creator.

Why the Swamp Metaphor

One afternoon Jim Watkins and I were in a meeting with a few others, discussing an activity as part of Atlanta's "Faith and the City" project. Jim was commenting on the plight in which pastors sometimes find themselves. He and I already had begun talking about the idea for this book, and Jim has a reputation among friends of coming up with colorful expressions. So when he ended his comment by saying, "It's like alligators in the swamp," something clicked inside of me. Without hesitation, I looked at him and said, "That's the title for our book!"

Admittedly, our most common impressions of alligators and swamps are second- and third-hand. Few of us have lived near a swamp or toured one; the closest that we get to alligators is from across a thick glass wall in a reptile house at the zoo. Yet images of swamps and alligators conjure up common stereotypes of this unique ecosystem and its most infamous inhabitants. In large part because we are not familiar with them, alligators and swamps seem to be very threatening to us humans. Swamps are not inviting, in terms of an easy place to visit. Only outlaws or recluses ever live in one. So why should a book about power and the church talk about such an important topic with such strange imagery? Seems a bit bizarre, yes?

Perhaps to a naïve, new pastor, but not to us. Pastors do not like to admit so in public, but in a pinch, they readily would assign the alligator and swamp metaphor to their "uncooperative" congregation and its apparent self-appointed powerbrokers. "Yes," these earnest but inexperienced children of the cloth would say, "my church truly is like a swamp sometimes; there are alligators and murky waters everywhere!" When someone feels powerless, it is easy to suppose that pictures of large eyes gliding through deceptively still water aptly apply—to someone else. In this book, we seek to use the alligator and swamp metaphor as widely as possible. In any given circumstance, at any point, anyone could be an alligator and any congregation could exhibit the more threatening features of a swamp. Pastors, deacons, music directors, Sunday school superintendents, church mothers, district superintendents, school principals, city council representatives, company presidents, mayors, governors all can be perceived by others as dangerous and demanding. Likewise, not only your congregation but your neighborhood, town, county, city, country club, service organization, or state could look to certain others as a veritable swamp. To some extent, alligators and swamps are in the eye of the beholder. The shifting capacity of this metaphor suggests that the *perception* of power—especially in menacing forms—can and does move as well.

Preview

It is to an informed savvy about power that this book is dedicated. Chapter two explores what is probably the most familiar contemporary object for understanding power: the self. We approach the self from the standpoint of voices traditionally absent from the chambers of power. Women and people of color tell a story of power that for so long has been silenced. Dr. Beverly Thompson, a spiritual director, pastoral counselor, and pastor, sensitively portrays this struggle for self and power in a way that speaks to all people of faith, regardless of gender or color. In this way, the deeper issues of the self's relationship to power are revealed most dramatically.

Yet, as we have seen from the summary of theories and definitions above, power is not framed simply in terms of the person. Power can be, and is, manifest in other human forms, too. Chapter three explores one of the forms that has not been understood well: that of culture. This approach does not, however, treat culture in terms of a list of content items, which differ from one group to another. Rather, culture here is laid out in terms of a "taxonomy," that is, an arrangement of categories that help to reveal culture's complexity. Borrowing again from the natural world, we will use metaphors. Culture is like both a swamp and streams of water meeting each other. As we see culture through these lenses, we begin to realize that culture is everywhere and, in today's American life, interacts in very subtle ways. Not only do we discover culture in our churches and their groups, we find it at our church doorsteps, in our towns and regions, and in general streaming throughout daily pathways. Learning to think about power in cultural terms helps, among other things, to de-personalize challenges in the church as well as beyond it.

Indeed, what is happening beyond your congregation's building has more bearing on its life than most church folks would care to admit. Dr. Harvey Newman, in chapter four, examines the life of cities and explains them in terms of a recent theory called regime politics. In this theory, no one network is in complete control all the time. City government, downtown big business, neighborhood groups, and others all jockey for position as various circumstances and issues present themselves. Dr. Newman shows how power can be exercised to make changes, even through a process known as "social learning." Furthermore, Newman argues persuasively that civic participation is a role that every congregation can undertake beneficially.

Chapter five draws our presentation of power back full circle. That is, power can be created and exercised, even by local citizens who would like to influence decisions that are made by government officials. Dr. Jim Watkins's chapter describes the work of public policy as a ministry. He draws upon his years as a pastor and as a staff person for a member of the U.S. Congress. His chapter offers many helpful ideas to practice in several forms of public ministry. Watkins also turns up the heat a bit, calling Christians to consider biblically and theologically the timely nature of vocation in today's public arena.

If power is a slippery eel in the swamp to identify and handle, then it is no surprise that leadership today struggles for a clear identity. Chapter six reflects upon the contributions of the previous four chapters and begins to draw them into a lucid approach to power. In

Okay, how do we get along with each other?

particular, the final chapter considers how the dynamics of power are involved in matters of change, abuse, religious behavior, and leadership itself. Power and leadership are not necessarily the same; too often they become separated, with the result that power gets exercised without leadership. We, as writers and persons of faith, believe that the best kind of leadership is that which persuades constructively, with integrity and wisdom. The final chapter will offer some suggestions on how people of faith can begin to live with power faithfully.

An Invitation

No one volume can speak to all the issues of its theme, and we will not pretend to do so. What we offer here is a resource that frames the conversation about power and church in a new way. By talking about power's complexity in nonjudgmental terms, we hope that pastors everywhere (along with their congregations) can become more effective in doing ministry. The world of the twenty-first century continues to become even more complicated. This complexity offers threat as well as promise. It is our hope that these discussions about power will stimulate further conversation, as well as fresh action. We commend the book to anyone in the church who seeks to be a steward of power.

It is our hope as well that the line illustrations both amuse and enlighten you. When I was very young, I remember learning to read with the *Curious George* and *The Cat in the Hat* series of books. As in all children's books, these series use attractive drawings to enhance the story. Once I reached college, book illustrations were few and far between. Seminary? Forget it! It was not until I began reading to my own child that I became aware, in a new way, of the power of the visual arts. As we writers prepared this book, we agreed that lighthearted illustrations would add to its usefulness. That child is now an adult, and she has provided here the drawings to enhance your reading and learning. If Christians cannot laugh at themselves as they grow in faith and witness, then surely we are a sorry lot, of limited use for God's purposes here. I have to believe that God has a wonderful sense of humor.

Think of the swamp as a place that you are headed out to visit for the first time. As with any new venture, you need certain items to make the trip safe, useful, and interesting. You will want to be dressed appropriately for being out on still water and in humid conditions. You will need travel tools for keeping your bearings—a compass and a map of the swamp (if there *is* one!). You will need to sit in a safe craft designed for transport in these conditions. Once you are on your way, you will rely upon proper travel gear, too—paddles, binoculars, drinking water, repellent, bird calls, pocket knife, etc. All of these items are necessary and increase the likelihood that your venture into the swamp will work out well.

We invite you, therefore, to join us on a fascinating journey into the swamp, the swamp of real life in the church and its world. What does this swamp look like? Beautiful, sometimes serene, busy in its own way, dangerous if you don't know your way around, but sustaining and rewarding when understood and engaged. We might not be able to change the swamp, but we can help it to fulfill its vocation within God's wider creation.

Self and "Dressing" for the Swamp: The Pastor as Alligator

by Beverly Thompson and
George B. Thompson, Jr.

2

Confessions of a Reluctant Alligator

D r. Beverly: As a woman of the South, I have to admit something: I don't want to shop for clothes to wear in a dreadful place like a swamp! When I think about myself in the role of "pastor as alligator"—well, as a faithful disciple so aptly put it so long ago—"Surely not I, Lord!" Swamps and alligators are not my style, not my way of imagining my call in pastoral ministry. Yet here I am, trudging through the day-to-day life of the church that I serve, and I have to admit that often it does feel like a swamp. It can be calm and beautiful one moment and disturbed by squabbling alligators the next moment. After a decade of pastoral ministry, I am more aware than ever that I need to remove the high heels and find more appropriate attire. Reluctantly, I acknowledge that there are ways to present myself that will be better suited to the world of the church swamp and its creatures around me.

Thinking about the pastoral role and how I "dress" for it leads me to realize that any discussion of power and the church needs to talk about self. What do pastors, elders, deacons, evangelists, Sunday school teachers, music ministers, youth advisors, and other church folks bring of themselves to their tasks? How does what I do as a pastor become interpreted by myself and others as an act of power—or the lack of it? How well do I understand myself and my own views of what power is? How do various views of human identity affect the way that churches and pastors engage power?

This chapter will help us to address issues of power in the church in terms of one's own self. Many books, both scholarly and popular, have been published over the years that talk about self. Americans have been inundated with theories of self, with self-help books on knowing yourself, feeling good about yourself, asserting yourself, actualizing yourself, and caring for yourself. This chapter does not try to treat all of these "self" topics. Its focus instead is upon awareness, attentiveness to the self that you are, and how your self deals with power in it and around it. Implied in the discussion is the idea that an attentive self is one that is learning and growing. Adults who respond to power the way they did as children are considered to behave inappropriately. They are not discovering more about themselves; they are not growing in their ability to manage themselves and relate with others effectively. In the metaphor of this book, they are not aware of the alligator in themselves.

Dr. Beverly: Like it or not, as a pastor, I am one of the alligators in the swamp of the church. My own self-understanding, no matter what it is, does affect how I see power and engage power. Employing tools like those described in this chapter provides me with a set of conceptual lenses and action tools to help myself and deal with others.

The Wardrobe in the Closet

Self-attentiveness, however, is influenced not simply by the nature of a person's humanity in general. In recent decades, society has begun to recognize the deep roles that gender and ethnic heritage have played as key factors in self and self-awareness. The two of us who contribute to this particular chapter bring different styles of clothing to our work. Although we both have experience as pastors, we enter the swamp from particular perspectives. A discussion of self and power in terms of gender and ethnic heritage will help all of us become more sensitive to complexities of power, even in the church. All of us then—female, male, black, brown, yellow, and white—can learn from one another. Then we will become better equipped to use the alligator in each one of us, for the good of us all.

On Changing Clothes

We will set our discussion with reflections in first person about particular experiences with power. In doing so, we will listen for four kinds of voices—female, male, African American, and Asian American. We will use these voices to help us think about power, to see power at work, to imagine and hope for power as a blessing rather than a curse. These voices will weave references to personal experience with broader, theoretical thinking. The value of this rhythm is to help the reader step back and consider self-awareness from more than one perspective. Varying voices help us realize that the common challenge of self-awareness is experienced in our society in various ways. Becoming sensitive to how other persons struggle with self-awareness might be hard at points for readers to face. Oppression as an evil can be subtle, even while it is so pervasive. We are convinced that it is worth being disoriented enough to learn what it takes to engage power.

Learning to be aware necessarily means thinking and acting in new ways. Our conversation with several voices will be followed by a look at a couple of tools designed for self-improvement. The PACE Profile is a compact resource that Dr. George Thompson has used for years in premarital counseling, social service training, and with hundreds of seminary students. Its insights equip men and women with a realistic, constructive way to improve self-awareness while becoming more skilled with others. This discussion of the PACE Profile dovetails closely with newer insights about leadership that build upon emotional intelligence. Primal leadership builds on brain research to suggest an interlocking set of skills that link self to others. Emotional intelligence proponents argue that a person cannot grow or lead without being in touch with what makes people tick at the deeper levels of human experience. The swamp of any church is filled with such deep beliefs and emotional convictions. While neither PACE nor primal leadership treats power as its central theme, it is always close by.

So, then, as we explore what is perhaps America's greatest obsession, we hope that the several angles on self in this chapter enrich every reader's ability to deal with power.

A Still, Small Voice

Dr. Beverly: I was born and raised in Atlanta, Georgia. My first awareness of God occurred in a Baptist church, where it became clear to me that this stern, male God had all the power but "he" had chosen to give a chunk of that power to my preacher. If my attire—that is to say, my way of working and living—was good enough, then that power was mildly benevolent. But the swamp is filled with all kinds of creatures; looking back, I think I lived those years sitting on the edge, my bare feet dangling into that murky water. God, humanity, and power held together in a lopsided, tenuous relationship.

Being the older of two daughters in a blue-collar family, I worked hard at finding ways to be me, of developing my own sense of self. I never thought much about who had what kind of power, especially in the church. One particular moment set off doubts in my heart. I walked down the aisle at Lakewood Heights Baptist Church one Sunday and told Rev. Rainwater that I believed God was calling me to be a pastor. The message from his response was loud and clear: God didn't use women like God could use men. So instead, I became the nurse that Rev. Rainwater said God was calling me to be. Then it began to occur to me that I must have been lacking something. That was about the time when I started thinking about this matter of self. Actually, to say I began thinking about self is a bit exaggerated. It is not so easy to think in terms of self, and it is just about as hard to define it.

Many students of the human person have sought to define what self is. One theological resource offers a general definition that would be accepted widely: "the concept of self is a structure of conscious and unconscious attitudes about the self, constituting a basic structure of personality, including self characteristics, self in relation to others, personal values and personal ideas and goals."[1] One secular psychologist argues that the ways in which the self may be defined are limitless.[2] We may see ourselves as women or men, tall or short, fat or skinny, bright or dense. Our "seeing" may have little to do with what others see when they look at us. What has become clear to me, though, is that this self is not a collection of ideas we dream up about our own selves; rather, these ideas exist in relationship to other persons. There is no such thing as self without relationship. Relationships provide experiences that influence our awareness of ourselves, including what kind of power is (or is not) available to us.

Self in Context

Let us consider this relational element further. Because of our relational nature, a person does not live in a single culture but in a series of cultures at any moment. These subcultures may consist of family, school, workplace, community, church, state, nation, or world. A person's self-concept is developed as a function of that subculture. As one moves from one subculture to another group or organization, that self-concept may no longer be consistent with the demands of the new group.[3] Thus, he/she may experience a loss of power. So, one's perception of self-power is not based internally as much as it is in response to others' demands.

Learning about self is also more than taking a snapshot of ourselves. As Robert Kegan submits, being a person is not something that happens to define me in the moment. It is who *I am*. I cannot look at this self because I am it. It is my own experience of self and of my power or powerlessness. For example, one might be a wife. It is what she is to think and how she is to act. It is how she experiences her sense of self and her sense of power. She cannot look at what being a wife means to her as a woman of a particular age with particular beliefs in a particular culture with particular fears and strengths because the only self she knows is the one she lives as "wife." It is how she defines her sense of self. It is her world. It is part of her social location. Each of us is located in a culture in which it is difficult to gain a perspective: It is the sum total of who one is, and each of us is always embedded somewhere at a particular moment of our lives.[4]

At the same time, one is capable of moving to a new balance out of that embeddedness that allows one to have a more full sense of self. In that movement, when one can begin to hear what one could not have even considered before, one's horizon begins to shift. It is at that point that transformation of sense of self becomes reality. One begins to claim a sense of self that acknowledges a powerfulness that can be used for the good of self and community. One is able then to move from an old way of powerlessness to a new way of being in relationship with any organization or community structure—even in the swamp!

Dr. Beverly: I know that my cultural bias is showing when I say that I do not see myself as a person of power. We Southern women don't talk about it. We see it and we know what it can do—to us, against us, and for us. We watch it being used not thinking about ways in which we use it too. What we do know is that women and men are socialized in most societies to deal with power differently. In what we can call the sociocultural narrative, we realize that culture tells us who we are before we ever begin to discover self. Boys are acculturated to be strong and powerful. Even today girls learn early in their lives that power is defined differently for them.[5]

One of my earliest memories of the reality of this social assumption was in grade school. My teacher, Mrs. Brown, suggested that I not run quite so fast because it's best to let the boys win. By the time that we reached high school, none of us girls ever thought about running in elections for president of anything at my high school. We were easily elected as vice-presidents and secretaries, but even then, our work was to support the boys who ran things.

The sociocultural narrative of gender and power also has been alive and well in the church's pastoral care of women. One female scholar, Riet Bons-Storm, illustrates this point dramatically, as she analyzes twenty-five case studies by one particular North American pastoral theologian.[6] Writing about the women, in ten of the seventeen cases, this male counselor/author uses the word "attractive" four times. In each one of these ten examples he mentions appearance each time, specifically noting something about their clothing, hairstyle, or body shape. However, none of the male case studies described the outer appearance of the male clients. Evidence like this should lead us to wonder about the continuing effects of male preference in society—and how it affects experiences of power.

What do I see when I look in the mirror?

Still, if you know anything about the culture of the church in the South, you know something about powerful women. Regardless of our ethnicity, it has always been the women who keep things surviving in the church. White women of the South are socialized to do whatever it takes to get things done but never to talk about the power it takes to do just that. It's what is known as the "steel magnolia syndrome." Like Scarlett O'Hara in *Gone With the Wind,* we use all of our wits to do what we believe must be done. Power? We women of the South just don't talk much about it.

Yet, beware! The alligator does rear her head from the swamp when threatened. In times of crisis, women often choose a mode of behavior contrary to the tradition-bound narrative. Many women are becoming more and more aware that they do not fit the self-narratives that have been dictated to them.

Surely we see that difference in the swamp of the church. When a woman feels called into ministry in the church, the sociocultural-dictated narrative no longer fits and the norm is challenged. A power struggle ensues. Carol A. Miles shares some troubling information about what happens when that norm is challenged.[7] Miles presents recent statistics of how few women serve as head of staff or solo pastors in the Presbyterian church (USA). In 2002, of 486 congregations with a membership of 800 or more, only ten of them were served by a woman. What does this fact say about the alligators in the swamp of the church?

Miles quotes Maxine Walaskay, a pastoral psychologist, who explains the ambivalence that congregations feel regarding a woman in the pulpit: "My hunch is that, even when they like what they hear, they feel ambiguous about what they see....When you get right down to it, it's just that 'I don't want a woman telling me what to do.'" [8]

Power, then, is not a foregone conclusion in the pastoral role, and this is especially true for women. Yet women in the pastoral role have to face alligators who pop up all over the swampland of the church.

Dr. Young Lee Hertig, an ordained minister and professor, writes about the power of Asian North American women, especially those who serve in professional roles in churches. She describes their struggle as one of "triple marginality—being a woman instead of a man, being the minority instead of the majority, and being marginalized among women."[9] Because North American Asian professional women find themselves estranged from both feminist movements and from their own ethnic groups, they seek affirmation from males rather than other females because these women perceive that men have the power. Young Lee shares the story of Wendy, a female ordained minister whose struggle is not unfamiliar to women in ministry:

People who do not know me treat me as a secretary and tell me to make copies for them. Once they find out that I am a pastor, they often cannot hide their surprise and do not know what to do with me. Unless I become a nationally known figure, this experience will continue. The flip side of this is in the case of a male. A friend of mine is not a pastor. Yet, with his tall height and gentle appearance, people call him a pastor. Ironically, he has yet to correct people that he is not a pastor.[10]

Wendy's story is a common one for female clergy of all ethnic backgrounds. The challenges of sterotypes—gender, race, age—becomes daunting for ordained women. Their situation personifies a thread in the American story of self and power.

Voices Waiting to Exhale

We need to be better equipped to spot power and powerlessness when it rears its head out of the water, as well as when it dives deep below the surface and refuses to come up for air. Sometimes that alligator blow knocks the breath out of us all—an experience that I call "the silencing of women." In that silencing, power shifts. We seem to have lost our voice and have become frighteningly quiet. At that moment, we alligators need resilient clothing and some trusted swamp creatures around to remind us who we are.

Dr. Beverly: I find that women spend a lot of time being quiet, even though few men would agree. In seeking to find my own true self, I have spent years as a nurse, gerontologist, counselor, spiritual director, and pastor. All along the way, I have spent time counseling women. I have found that often women cannot express their feelings to a pastor or a pastoral counselor because they have been silenced by the powerful alligators around them. They can find no acceptable words to speak. Feelings of discontent and the desire to be more than who others think they should be remain hidden deep within them. This phenomenon further isolates women from one another and from those to whom they go for help. Hence, their ability to experience power continues to be stunted.

It is actually not that the women do not speak at all. Rather, they choose their words carefully, and their truth often lies hidden. When a woman says that she can no longer be the wife, mother, pastor she has been for years, pastors, pastoral counselors, and spiritual directors have difficulty listening. Often we cannot hear the words as cries for power because they stir uneasy emotions within us. Women often feel powerless to speak about their hidden conflicts, desires, or frustrations with life as it is because they fear losing the esteem of others. Therefore, they are silent—or perhaps more accurately, they are silenced.

How can we of the church listen to the silenced voice of the woman who feels powerless? Often we do not. Our fears just keep on silencing others and often even affirm their powerlessness. We find subtle ways to remind her of her responsibilities to be the good wife, the strong mother, the good pastor. We cannot allow ourselves to imagine what would happen in our own daily lives if our own spouse or, heaven forbid, even our very own being were to be summoned out and discover the voice of power within. However, it is also important that the silence be treated as a time of listening. Pastors, counselors, and spiritual directors need to be aware that there is a difference between silence and silenced voices. Those in the midst of an alligator attack do need a safe silent space to "be." What many women need is a sacred space for their silence. Eventually, at the kairos moment, they will be ready for more appropriate clothing to reenter the climate of the swamp.

Let me reiterate: Silence in itself is not a bad thing. Being silenced and staying silenced because of the power of another person or an oppressive society, however, is deadly.

Dr. Beverly: Some time ago, as members of a Transitions Group I facilitated struggled to find self, we turned to Job. The Book of Job, even with its absence of alligators and swamps, nevertheless says a lot about both power and silenced voice. These insights were helpful to the women in the transition group. The promising element of Job's breaking silence is that he did it. Finally Job speaks out of his pain and claims for himself a different kind of personal power. It looks like Job trusted the friends who stayed with him long enough to finally find his voice and speak of his pain out loud. In the Transitions Group, a deep level of trust was necessary before any of the women was able to find her voice. Even in this small group, there was fear of alligators.

Eventually Sarah, who had chosen not to join into our conversations or prayers, and who had expressed a dislike for journaling (a necessary tool for all members of this group), was able to speak out of her silence. On this particular evening she asked if she might read a bit of her journal to the group. This faithful woman read several pages of her personal suffering and pain. She claimed her powerlessness as finally she claimed her plight: widow. Her journaling took the form of great lament as the other women sat in the circle and listened.

Sarah had tried to express her pain and powerlessness in other settings, with other people, even her family, but to no avail. It is difficult to hear the voiced pain of powerlessness. Often the ones who finally do hear can't listen to the anger and frustration that is named by the weakened alligator. Instead, they try to silence her. When this happens, all the Sarahs remain muted in isolation, unable to crawl back into the swamp.[11]

It might seem difficult and even painful to acknowledge that the self's experience of power is deeply affected by whether one is male or female. It is just as painful to acknowledge that power is deeply affected by racial and ethnic heritage. Put the two factors together and you have a story that is sometimes too hard to bear.

An African American View

Teresa L. Fry Brown, writing from the Womanist perspective, shares these words from silenced women she met in discussion group: "You keep talking about finding your own voice; we can't even breathe!" Brown says that African American women have learned to breathe on stolen air, silently so that no one could detect their presence.[12] Silenced women experience powerlessness. I have seen many women turn inward and become depressed while others become isolated. Most run from pastorates and find other ways of serving God and humanity. Unfortunately, many are referred for medical treatment, especially medication.

These women cannot find words to break their silence alone. Female pastors have to be strong alligators. Nobody should see them limping through the swamp or they just might be dragged deep below. Yet finally they drag their wounded tails to the banks of the swamp in one last-ditch effort to survive. Still, we pastors and pastoral counselors often remain unable to hear whatever words they form when and if they form them. We behave more like the "friends" of Job who, rather than hearing, speak words which we believe will bring hope. But the women remain silenced —and powerless.

The powerlessness of women—the not knowing how to claim power or react to power in a productive way—often comes to us from a misreading of biblical texts about power. When Jesus speaks about turning the other cheek to our enemies (Matthew 5:39), too often women read these words as a Christian call to be passive against one's aggressor. But there is another way of reading this well-known passage that is more hermeneutically faithful. Walter Wink suggests that in the first century, the act of turning one's head and offering one's other cheek would have been viewed as an act of resistance. It would have indicated to the aggressor that you were turning the tables on her or him. In other words, resistance also can mean utilizing actions toward the aggressor on terms other than those which the aggressor defines.[13] All along these lines, then, powerless women can discover power in themselves if they learn to be creative about their resistance. They can do so on the basis of fresh insights about the Bible.

Women Sniffing Power

However, lest we become too comfortable in these new pieces of swamp dress, we ought to hang a warning in the swamp that reads: "Careful! Power begets power." As the alligator claims power, it becomes tempting to become a carrier of the power-abuse of the big gators in the swamp who now want to take you in. We hear stories of women who fight the power-gators using various tools, only to claim that power for themselves and begin to abuse it, just like the big gator before them.

Other women choose to stay away from places where they might be able to use their power in a positive way because they are unwilling to become "like the big gators." That kind of dress won't help anybody stuck in the swamplike place known as church. It becomes a place on the edge, a marginal, liminal place where it is easy to look in and criticize, but just as easy to stay out. I agree with another Womanist theologian, Rosita deAnn Mathews, Director of Chaplaincy in a veterans' administration hospital, who says, "Marginality is also never safe, for one lives in fear that the power from the center will come to the margin to consume it."[14] Selves seeking power must learn to weigh risks as they move from the margins.

As pastors living in the swamplike world of the church, we have some work to do as we dress for the part. We cannot live out our calling as ministers of word and sacrament running from alligators all around us. Rather, we have to find ways to dress appropriately for the swamp. One of the keys is developing an awareness of our own self, of how we tend to operate, what we value, how we respond to stress, how we have come to terms with our own disappointments and accomplishments. Self-attentiveness prepares us better to swim in the swamp in spite of the churning that seems to happen there over and over.

Resisting Force

Mathews suggests that the response to the aggressive power of another is not one of passivity but of denying the aggressor the opportunity to define our method of resistance. Echoing Walter Wink, she writes, "Resisting evil requires one to fight evil, but not on its terms....Do not use evil to fight evil."[15] This kind of response was used widely in the Civil Rights movement. It calls for enough self-awareness and discipline to overcome our natural tendency to want to hurt those who hurt us.

So, what if we alligator pastors are wise enough about who we are called to be to use our own power to resist the threat of another creature? What if we are able to do so by maintaining or establishing ethical principles and moral standards and refusing to employ the aggressor's methods? Mathews calls this kind of response to aggression "using power from the periphery."[16] If both male and female alligators serving God in the swamp of the church could know themselves well enough and find their own voices, the pastorate could be a genuine countercultural model following the Jesus we meet in scripture. Power from the periphery forces us to know our own selves, to think and plan our responses to attack, and to respond with integrity and power for the sake of the cause of Christ.

Rosita Mathews also fits us with more appropriate swamp attire as she teaches us how to dress operating from the periphery. She speaks of setting limits as to what kinds of interactions we will participate in if a system or a person chooses to use power against others. She reminds us that:

Through the denial of its power (the system) over us, we find that we become more powerful...those in the center of an abusive system become symbiotically tied to the system and dependent on its power for their life. Those on the outside of the system, the periphery, gain strength from other places of power in order to exist. We search our souls, our experiences, our relationships—that is, our lived faith—for inner resources of such strength.[17]

It is beginning to look like we need a variety of attire for life in the swamp. Perhaps one of the outfits looks a bit like reclaiming our ability to be a woman as a gift of God's grace. African American author Patricia Hunter writes:

Reclaiming our womanhood and our ability to be womanish as a gift of God's grace is a painful and painstakingly slow process. Part of the pain lies in realizing a systemic conspiracy has been at work to prevent women of color from knowing their power and passion. ...Each tool of oppression and prejudice must be confronted and dismantled. It is reasonable to turn to other women who have been isolated, marginalized, and oppressed to join us in demanding release.[18]

What's an alligator to wear?

Dressing for grace, then, does not necessarily mean that life in the swamp will be easy.

We cannot deny that, like many other societies that have existed in history, American society has oppressed peoples. Forms of oppression continue today, in spite of various efforts to create a fully free society. Oppressed selves struggle to deal with power in ways that do not harm themselves or others. Those of us who live with more privilege than oppression are called by the Gospel to face the evil ways that power is used. Such a task calls for a deeper examination of oneself. At the same time, regardless of the pain and oppression that many others have endured in their lives, they never will be effective with power until they can face through a centered self their own abuse by power.

A Voice in Appearance Only?

Dr. George: My experience of many things has been heavily shaped by life in the Pacific Northwest. All of my youth, and the early part of my adult life, were spent there, in the fall drizzles, the winter's wet greyness, and the late summer's glorious dry sunshine. It was in gazing at volcanic peaks in the Cascades Range that I first became conscious of the majesty of God and of my place as a creature made to praise my Creator. In some vague ways I suppose that those epiphanic moments also left me with feelings about power—the power of the natural world, of the wonder of God, and the call to yield oneself, in spite of sin, through trust to the One who not only creates but redeems and sustains as well. Making a conscious choice to be a "follower of the Way" seemed in my earnest youth to renounce power, not claim it. Power, I supposed, was selfish, sinful, and ultimately destructive. Feelings like these still arise in me when I visit those mountains.

In chapter one, I write briefly of several childhood and youthful experiences of power of various sorts. As a father, I sought to encourage my young daughter to experience positive accomplishments so that she would grow up feeling that she was capable and worthwhile. If this were a book on child psychology or parenting, it would be fitting to explore the relationships between accomplishment, esteem, power, and self-understanding. Perhaps the most important notion out of my personal reflections is that participating in social privilege does not guarantee that a person learns how to use power (let alone to use power beneficially). American society must continue to make a place for everyone at the table; this is a goal about sharing power.

At the same time, ironically, there are a lot of persons who bear the trappings of power but the wounds of powerlessness. Many of them are male and white. They bear not-so-hidden scars of attacks on the banks of the swamp. I once was forced to resign a job by two women who were younger than me. My age and gender provided no protection.

One of the reasons I think that power continues to be abused in today's world is that boys and men keep getting the message that power is force. Images of aggression—athletic, military, social—

remain the dominant pictures for how "real men" behave. A male self is a "take-charge" self, independent, confident, accomplished. What happens to boys when "power over" is their only image of self? What happens to society?

Dr. George: What I have not been as aware of in my life is how significant certain kinds of power have been available to me because of my gender and skin color. It is not that I have had many moments in my life where I felt powerful. To the contrary: my feeling powerful has been fairly limited, if by powerful one means influential or able to impose one's will upon others. Being a student government officer probably was my clearest experience of power for many years. Certainly my pastoral experiences bear little or none of this kind of power, except for the freedom to select biblical texts for preaching (and bear the consequences of the subsequent sermon). Rather, I left all but one of my pastoral situations feeling as though I had accomplished little that would benefit the congregation in the long run. As a pastor, any sense of exercised power on my part ended up thwarted or misguided.

To grow in self-awareness, to be able to engage power both faithfully and usefully, American men need to struggle with how society's primary images of being a self are limited. It seems that our society's ever-growing mania with sports only underscores the problem. You are "somebody," you are powerful only if you are athletic, highly skilled, and win against someone else. Add to that the legacy of racism, and white males strangely symbolize the struggle for a just society, not to mention of greater personal self-awareness. As white boys and white men face their own failures in light of the dominant myths of power, they will need as much encouragement as anyone else who struggles. It might be the case that society will not learn to share power until it frees majority males of the tyranny of aggression as self-worth. Alligators have to learn to get along.

In other words, let us demonstrate, especially to those most susceptible to the dominant model, that power and self can be experienced differently—and better. Let us help boys and the majority white population to engage power in ways that respect others and expand power. The more that such a venture works, the more that the voicelessness of women can be overcome. The more that such a venture works, the more fully will people of color be included. When all members of society are free to participate, we are more likely to foster citizens whose self-awareness creates power that helps, not hurts. Alligators who let the beavers, the herons, and the snakes also enjoy the swamp use their power for the common good.

Voices and Voicelessness

Racial/ethnic experiences with power, introduced above, can instruct all of us about self in another way. By comparing how behaviors in one culture are interpreted in another culture, we become more aware of how self is deeply affected by culture. Eric Law's writings on multicultural ministry offer a wonderful source of insight along these lines.[19] As a Chinese American, Law is able to perceive how Western and Asian societies interpret certain interpersonal actions differently. His experience as a student, first in Hong Kong and then in the United States, illustrates this point.[20] In Hong Kong, a student prepares for class so that when the teacher calls on the student, she or he is able to provide the requested information. In the United States, the teacher asks a question of the class and then waits for an answer. The tendency is for a few students to dominate the time available for discussion, thus eliminating the chance for every student to say something. Those who speak up usually are viewed as the motivated and intelligent ones, while the ones who never say anything are perceived as dull and lazy. In Hong Kong, this pattern of behavior would be seen as quite odd and inappropriate.

Dr. George: What happens, then, to an Asian immigrant who begins an American school and waits in class for the teacher to call on her for the answer? Her polite silence is interpreted by the Americans as timidity, lack of preparation, or, worse yet, stupidity. At home in Hong Kong, her silent readiness was honored with attention from the teacher, and she thus experienced personal power in a positive way. In the United States, her silence is viewed as a lack of confidence and of personal power, leading to possible ridicule and rejection. One pattern of behavior in two varying cultural contexts leads to conflicting messages about self and power. In such a situation, growing young alligators don't know what to think.

Dr. George: The backdrop of my life—and that of most white males, I would venture to suggest—put me in positions to benefit from opportunities that afford power. I have been able to receive a high degree of formal education, putting me in the top one-tenth of one percent of the U.S. population. I have been free to buy houses and secure mortgages without difficulty. I have been able in many (but not all) employment applications to be considered on the basis of my merit. I can and do move in society's public arena with little particular concern for my well-being and treatment by others. In all of these ways, being white and being male traditionally have been advantageous; in my life, they have worked as invisible privileges to my benefit. On the surface, I appear to fit in with other alligators.

Law's discussion of "power distance" also demonstrates how individuals in different cultural contexts perceive power in vastly different ways. Drawing upon the research of Geert Hofstede, Law argues that persons who hail from certain nations tend to perceive themselves with little personal power—"high power distance." Those from other nations, mostly Western, perceive themselves and others as having considerable personal power—"low power distance." When immigrant communities in the United States hail from high-power-distance nations, their view of self and power does not correspond to the cultural context in which they now live. Natives of the United States might interpret these immigrants' deferential behavior as weak and indecisive, not realizing that their cultural training about self is different. Cultural misunderstandings confuse everyone and complicate development of self. Ethnic persons who are at ease with negotiating various kinds of power have learned how to navigate between the swamps of their home culture and those of wider society.[21]

Let us restate the main points of the chapter so far. Issues of self with white men, white women, African American women, and cross-cultural comparisons all provide us pause as we consider the meanings of self and power. Who are you, and what power is available to you? The answer to these questions might not be as straightforward as it first seemed. Perhaps you usually feel powerful or—just the opposite—powerless. Your perceptions, we are suggesting in this chapter, are influenced not merely by your being an individual person but also by your being located somewhere in particular, socially and culturally. Men and women usually have experienced these effects upon self very differently. So have people of color in America. As the United States becomes increasingly diverse, these questions will continue to be challenging. Chapter three will explore cultural categories and power in more detail. In this chapter, we continue to circle our discussion around the matter of the self who must learn to deal with power, internally and externally.

Dr. George: So what happens to someone like me when the backdrop does not match up with what appears to be the action in the scene? What happens to my sense of self when, as I pursue my Christian vocation, I keep experiencing the sensation of hitting a brick wall (or a big marshmallow—in either case, you eventually stop moving)? What happens to my identity, my self-esteem, my capacity for power, when I perceive that my efforts to engage power are ignored or resisted? Does the fact that I am a white male automatically negate my sense of negation? Or is power a more nuanced phenomenon than all that?

Whether we find it easy, difficult or confusing to engage power, none of us is immune from the frustration and confusion of doubting ourselves and our capacities. People who lead know how to use power appropriately, which means that they have developed good handles on self-wisdom. Insight alone does not change us. Let us therefore look at resources that anyone can use to enhance their potential with power.

Becoming More Self-Aware

During the twentieth century, human beings learned—among many other things—various ways to measure characteristics of the self. Among many "personality tests" and related instruments designed to help people understand themselves and function better, the PACE Profile [22] is one of the most useful. Since it is not long and not based upon depth psychology, PACE has been used with all kinds of people in all kinds of settings. Its purpose is to provide information about personal-style preference matched with practical behavior management skills. The overall design of the profile illustrates one of the claims of this chapter: namely, that self-awareness leads to more skill with others.

Pacing Ourselves

PACE organizes its measurement along four clusters of behaviors, four general ways out of which persons seem to prefer to function. There are no right or wrong, better or worse styles in PACE; your own particular style preference is just that—yours. Some people discover that they use one style almost exclusively; others shift from one to another depending on the circumstances. Behavior patterns sometimes shift when a person moves from operating out of feeling centered to feeling distressed or troubled. The important starting point is to find out what one's own profile inventory looks like.

One of the four styles operates with a concern for figuring things out before acting. The person who uses this style tends to appear quiet because they are gathering information and processing it. She or he tends not to be impulsive or emotional since they spend their energy putting plans together and following them. This person, then, can work alone happily and follow comfortable routines. This style is the "P" in the PACE acronym; it stands for "Predicting." To a group of others, the Predicting style offers a mild-mannered temper with focused attention upon details and process. These are strengths that any group needs at given moments.

What happens, however, to someone who uses this style when they are upset? All of the characteristics that can be used productively begin to work more intensely, which leads to "gumming up the works." The analytical concern continues to seek even more information, which slows everything almost to a halt. The distressed person using this style seems uninterested and even mentally "checked out" of the situation. He or she does not want to change anything and will dig in heels if pushed. What has happened to the self in Predicting overload? It has lost track of its ability to utilize information and process to get something accomplished—i.e., to use power well.[23]

A second style preference does not focus upon tasks, as does the Predicting style, but rather upon relationships. The person who uses this style clearly is interested in the comfort and satisfaction of others. She or he senses how others feel and has learned how to reduce tension in strained circumstances. In so doing, the person using this style puts their own concerns and needs to one side and adapts. This "A" style, for "Attending," clearly contributes to a group by helping it to work together.

What happens, however, to someone who uses the Attending style when they are upset? Their social radar gets out of whack; they don't like the heat and they want to get out of the kitchen. They will make promises but not follow through. Perhaps worst of all for the person, he or she loses track of personal wants. So, what has happened to the self in attending overload? It has lost track of itself, it senses no voice, and it has no access to power.[24]

A third style preference in the PACE Profile behaves like the Predicting style as it focuses upon tasks and likes working alone. Unlike Predicting, however, this third style is oriented not to analysis but to action. Persons who naturally use this style are often seen as leaders because they want to get things done. (When my daughter was ten or eleven, she came home from school and was describing a project with which she was heavily involved, confessing in a moment of candor that "I like to tell people what to do.") They usually exude energy, optimism, risk-taking, poise, and can motivate others to action as well. This style is the "C" of PACE, the "Conducting" style. It provides a group with important energy, direction, and a sense of accomplishment.[25]

Yet, every style has its Achilles' heel if it is not managed well. When those who use Conducting style are feeling stressed out, the useful qualities of their behavior turn somewhat monstrous. They want to get their way, their voices speak faster and louder, they see less and less of the bigger picture, they run over other people and their contributions, and they take on too much. On top of all this, the person using the Conducting style in distress usually has no idea of the effect that they are having on others. What has happened to the self in Conducting overload? It has turned the situation into a personal display of power, which all too often leaves everyone else feeling stripped of any of their power.

A fourth, final style preference in the PACE instrument focuses upon relationships and teamwork, as does the Attending style. What is distinctive in this fourth style, however, is its concern for high ideals. Often known as the perfectionist, this style wants things to be right. The person using this style during times of positive energy will commit tremendous time and resources to something that he or she deeply believes is important. Along the way, this person will give much of themselves to the project and to encouraging the group. As the "E" in PACE, this "Excelling" style stimulates a group to do its best.

As with all the other styles, however, the Excelling style does change its behavior and effectiveness when it goes over the edge. These behavioral changes are the most dramatically different of all four styles, for the person using Excelling in distress experiences a great change of countenance. Now everything is either good or bad, one way or the other, with no nuances or subtleties. The gap between cherished ideals and the current reality (as perceived) triggers Excelling-style persons to feel very let down, discouraged, and critical. No one is getting it right, least of all themselves. Self-criticism becomes intense and spirals downward if the distress continues over a period of time. So, what has happened to the self in Excelling overload? It is in danger—not simply of being lost, but of being destroyed by itself, of disintegrating its own power potential.[26]

An instrument like the PACE Profile can be valuable for self-understanding in a number of ways. For one thing, as mentioned earlier, it is simple enough to be used widely, since it is not as complicated as many other instruments (e.g., the MBTI names sixteen temperaments, Enneagram names nine). For another, it links strengths and weaknesses together as two sides of the same style coin. This upbeat way of conceiving personal problems has seemed to me over the years to be a more constructive way of dealing with most people who are trying to grow. A third way that PACE is useful is that it links insights and skills at two levels, for oneself and in relationships.

In this regard, PACE becomes a rich resource for developing the kind of leadership that Daniel Goleman bases on emotional intelligence.[27] Because leadership and power relate so closely, developing emotional intelligence becomes a critical step in learning to manage their own alligator and the alligator in others.

According to Goleman and associates, emotionally intelligent people have learned how to be effective in two sets of skills: attentiveness to themselves and to relationships, and regulation of themselves and of relationships. A learner of oneself develops the capacity to learn about others, to tune into their concerns and needs. Furthermore, one who disciplines oneself to become more open, controlled, flexible, functional, and the like also is better able to bring such skills into relationships with others. For Goleman and associates, the sequence of growth begins with self-awareness, moving to self-management, then social awareness, and finally relationship management.[28] The resources of the PACE Profile do just this. They provide hands-on tools for self-insight, self-regulation, and then extend to insights and productive interactions with others.

In light of continued social injustices, a discussion of skills for personal and social management is not irrelevant. Think about the effect that Mahatma Gandhi and Dr. Martin Luther King, Jr., have had on the world. They could not have led movements for independence and civil rights without knowing well who they were as persons— fears, warts, and all. Furthermore, they could not have been effective without knowing how to manage relationships with others. Both of them met fierce resistance, and both paid for their efforts with their lives. Surely, we who seek to use power for good do not automatically face the prospect of assassination. Yet, if what we seek to accomplish indeed matters, we have to face within our own selves any fears that inhibit us from finding our voices. Gandhi and King did not grow up deciding to die for a cause. Early in their lives, they faced their own inner, queasy qualms. They managed somehow to find the voice that would help them dress for the dangerous swamp that they deliberately entered. It was a swamp full of power and resistance. Their self-awareness, self-management, social awareness, and relationship management combined to stimulate their engagement of power. Surely any of us can learn the same insights and skills as we face on any given day the power all around us.

Power and You

This chapter has treated the theme of self and power from more than one particular vantage point. Rather than assuming that there is one universal way to frame the question, we approached the matter by offering voices about gender and ethnic heritage. Some of that discussion has been heavy since it seeks to name the lack of power and self-understanding that women and ethnic groups often experience.

I am somebody, too!

Yet their vantage points can serve to highlight the challenge for any-one: that you can't use power well until you have worked through your own stuff. There are many ways to do that work and link it with skill development. As personal resources, one's own skills then become potent, able to generate power when circumstances encourage or call for it. One way that society will become more just is through mature, self-aware women and people of color claiming power with tools that they have learned, sometimes against the odds. Alligators who use power for good are alligators who learn, practice, and put their acquired skills to use, not merely for themselves.

Chapter three will lay out an extensive cultural model of power that emphasizes the influence upon self of the deeper trappings of community. That chapter also discusses Eric Law's model, the Cycle of Gospel Living, that addresses power-sharing at a group level. In a sense, then, we will be looking at the flipside of the discussion that began here.

Dressing for the swamp of your church's culture means that you need to know what you have in your closet and what you are carrying in your suitcase. From what sources did these clothes come? What purposes did wearing them serve? Some of the ones that you have been carrying might not fit right or send the right message. How will you know this? Have you looked in the mirror lately to get a picture of how you are coming across? What does the alligator that you see there look like? Alligators who help the swamp are alligators who know who they are, what they can do, and with whom they get along. They know where they are when they seek to use power. Perhaps most of all, they contribute to the life and health of the entire swamp. Whether you are a big alligator, a little alligator, one with false eyelashes, or new to the swamp, your best bet with power is by beginning with yourself.

Maps and Compass:
Swamp Culture and Power

by George B. Thompson, Jr.

3

"Yes, Pastor, There Is a Swamp!"

Once a pastoral colleague of mine and I were talking church business. He was serving on a committee that oversees relationships between congregations and their pastors. That committee had met recently, and it was clear that my colleague was distressed by something. "We had another two situations come up at the meeting where we had to help a pastor negotiate a severance agreement with the congregation," he recounted to me. "When I was driving home, I counted up how many pastors have left their positions in the last year alone, less than two years after beginning their calls at those churches. Ten! In the last year! Those pastors hardly had gotten started, and their churches wanted them gone!"

Sinking in the Mud

This story is hardly unique. Every year hundreds of pastors leave their pastoral positions under difficult and draining circumstances. Many of them are fired, some find another church first and then leave (which always "looks better" for both parties), while still others muddle through some sort of negotiated departure. I know how painful these situations can be since I have experienced it more than once myself as a pastor. Three times in a row in my pastoral searches, I took great efforts to learn what the congregation was like and to represent myself accurately. In every situation, once I arrived, I ran into dynamics that I did not see coming. I went through what became an almost predictable process of feeling confused, mistreated, and very discouraged. By the time the third pastorate concluded, I had serious doubts about my ability to understand a church adequately. Perhaps more dishearteningly, I felt stripped of my dignity since I could not accomplish what I had set out to do. I was feeling not only like a failure; I was impotent, powerless.

Whatever the details of the exit scenario, pastoral departures like these should serve as a signal of danger. A lot of energy gets used up when pastors and churches are not happy with each other. All of the persons involved try to use whatever power they can muster to their advantage. Misunderstandings that lead to disagreements, that lead to contests, that lead to "winning" and "losing," end up being good neither for the pastor nor for the congregation. In the long run, the Gospel witness of both parties is jeopardized, and that should concern everyone involved.

Chapter two has helped us think about how pastors are alligators. A pastor who is not in touch with her or his own capacity for power cannot utilize it appropriately. The metaphor of "voice" in chapter two gives us a vivid way to emphasize the challenges of self and power. Admittedly, some segments of American society long have lived with strong limits to the kinds of power that were available to them. Powerless persons who learn how to speak are clothing themselves with what it takes for any person to engage power. There are contexts in which virtually anyone can become an alligator.

The present chapter looks at the alligator metaphor from the other side. Alligators live in swamps, and if they do not know the swamp in which they reside, they are in trouble. Any one of us can be an alligator, and all of us live in the swamp. It is not inappropriate at all, therefore, to think of the world of parish ministry as a swamp. Swamps have a beauty all their own, born out of the complex and fragile ecosystem that they are and upon which they depend. Unique plants and animals live there. Much of the time things appear quiet, as the various creatures go about the rhythm of seasons to take care of themselves. To the outsider, the occasional observer, the swamp could seem quite benign and even most inviting.

Yet, as we know, alligators and swamps have tended to be interpreted in dangerous and negative language. As a phenomenon of nature, a swamp rarely gets the kind of good press that, say, a beautiful mountain landscape does. A bucolic swamp scene can be quickly interrupted by the sudden movement of its most feared creature, the alligator. That long snout and those rows of sharp teeth elicit fear among human onlookers, as beady eyes appear to seek out a meal from any moving source. So it might seem odd or even insulting to suggest that those of us who fulfill our vocations in congregations perhaps (to risk mixing metaphors) have jumped off the deep end!

Claiming the Swamp

At a glance, swamps do not seem to be nearly as complex, mystifying, and potentially hazardous as they actually are. For pastors, the swamp of a new congregation could appear deceptively attractive, so much so that the nature of the swamp as a swamp might disappear well below the surface of the water. Similarly, pastors new to ministry often see themselves (or, perhaps more problematically, are viewed by churches) as defenseless creatures who do not know the terrain. It is easy for idealistic new pastors to feel picked on and be eaten alive by alligators! If a pastor does not know that she has entered a swamp, she probably will not have the right navigation equipment with her for her journey of ministry there. She might also incorrectly assume that the only potential threats to the swamp will come from someone else—never herself!

Getting Our Bearings

We have seen already how important it is for pastors to understand themselves and their own qualities and inclinations as alligators. If you don't believe that you are an alligator, you probably have bitten off someone's head and didn't know it! Yes, pastors can be and are alligators—and the same is true for church members. The particular ways in which alligators function depend upon the swamp and the alligator's ability to know how to get around it. One of the dynamics that gets pastors in trouble is assuming that the swamp that they have just entered (i.e., a new congregation) works the same way as the one they just left. Yet, is this ever the case, truly? If you think so, you are setting yourself up to bring out the worst in your own alligator—and in everyone else's, too. As a pastor and teacher, I believe that much of the struggle over and the misuse of power is directly related to operating frameworks in alligators' heads that are inadequate for the situation. In other words, we get in trouble with each other because we don't understand fully enough what is going on.

Our framework for interpreting the world of the swamp is one that seeks to make up for the limited effectiveness of models that we commonly use. This new framework is that of culture. By culture, we mean—in the simplest of terms—"shared meaning and behavior."[1] Below, we will spell out several key sets of concepts for understanding the presence and dynamics of culture. Cultural anthropology as a discipline has existed for more than a century and often is associated with Western research on third world villages. Yet application of anthropological method and theory to many other areas of human experience has expanded significantly in the last generation. These concepts are richly promising as analytical—as well as practical—resources for churches. Those introduced here derive primarily from recent research and writing on organizational culture.[2]

Cultural Claims That Influence Power

So, in this chapter, we will work with certain terms and see how they help us understand the intricate cultural world of parish ministry. We then will consider pastoral ministry in terms of culture as power. Simply put, culture is the swamp within which alligators navigate and negotiate their lives. Along the way, we will argue directly or indirectly for the following claims about culture:

1. Culture is complex, much more so than we usually realize.

One of my strongest impressions as a teacher and trainer for congregations is that we significantly oversimplify the nature of the phenomenon. That is, we tend to suppose that interpretations of congregational events and experiences are adequate if they follow some rubric out of psychology, traditional business management, or doctrinal perspective. As a result, ordained and active lay people vastly underestimate the complexity of church dynamics. This is especially true when a disagreement begins to escalate into a conflict.[3]

Like any human organization, churches behave in much more intricate ways. Issues of status, division of labor, reward, power, and so on usually do not yield to explanations that appear straightforward. This is why a discipline like cultural anthropology can be so useful in understanding church and power. Culture itself emerges in nuanced ways that even longtime members of the group do not completely understand, even as they intuitively accept how it functions. Simply put, there is more than meets the eye! This is a lesson that baby alligators need to learn early on if they are going to survive in the swamp.

2. Culture is essential to the exercise of power.

Once we recognize how culture permeates our church life so thoroughly, it becomes easier to explore its connections with power. Indeed, the indirect argument here is that, because culture is poorly misunderstood, church folks rarely consider it significant. Hence, it does not occur to most of us that culture itself could be a source of power. By the end of this chapter, relationships between cultural dynamics and the exercise of power should be more evident.

3. Culture contains decisive elements that are hidden from immediate view.

This claim flows out of the first one. It contends that culture cannot be completely understood by paying attention only to elements that are readily observable. Instead, the primary reason that culture is not easy to understand is that its very foundational factors rest hidden from view. This mysterious but bona fide quality is why I find the analogy of a swamp such a helpful tool for teaching about culture. We will explore this swamplike quality of culture shortly.

4. Because of culture, power is not readily channeled into democratic processes.

Americans grow up inculcated into a society that promotes the ideals of voice and vote for every citizen. We are taught as children to believe that each person has a right to speak about issues of common concern and to elect our government officials. As we will see in this chapter, these kinds of beliefs do indeed play a role in culture, but they do not tell the whole story. Culture itself is more elusive than its stated ideals.

What this cultural depth means for power is quite noteworthy. Consider, for instance, the experiences that the United States has undergone in recent years as its military forces got involved in countries like Afghanistan and Iraq. As the major phases of the military operations appeared to be drawing to a close, official rhetoric shifted from tactical summaries to declarations on the part of the U.S. State Department about long-term political intent. The United States now sought to help these countries establish democratic governments, a way of life in distinct contrast to tyrannies of dictatorship or tribal factiousness.

However, changing a country's way of life is not easy. While the visible structures through which power is exercised might be different, that people's cultural dynamics usually remain virtually intact. As an ideal to be seriously applied, democracy is a relatively recent phenomenon in the world. Forms of government that do not allow for free speech and suffrage express cultures in which power is more concentrated. It will take decades of concerted attention and effort before places like Afghanistan and Iraq actually live by democratic ideals.

This same difficulty occurs between churches, pastors, and their communities. Just because a church exists in America does not necessarily mean that the culture of the congregation believes deeply in democracy. As a student of and teacher about congregations, I know that this is the case: Power in churches rarely follows an agreed-upon procedure of wide participation. To recognize this reality is the beginning of wisdom about the relationship between power and its cultural bases.

5. Culture links every congregation, in one way or another,
   to its community.

Recent research in congregational studies emphasizes the integral ties that affect the prospects of a congregation in its particular setting.[4] Up until the massive mobility made possible by automobiles, local churches were established by the people who lived fairly close to each other and who constructed buildings in walking distance of their homes. As long as the same constituency of people continued to live in that community, the culture of that community—

and the culture of that church—would remain pretty much the same. In rural areas, this kind of stability was standard. In the growing American cities, however, migrations of ethnic and class groups from one neighborhood to another upset the church-community ties.

For instance, a working-class white Methodist church might be thriving in a stable city neighborhood. Its cultural values widely reflect those of many (but not necessarily all) of the area's residents, making church growth fairly straightforward. As the years go by, however, children of the Methodist church begin to move away, seeking greener pastures in newer suburban communities. Eventually, the housing stock in that neighborhood begins to be inhabited by people whose ethnic and cultural backgrounds have little in common with those brought by the working-class white Methodists. These new residents often do not feel welcome or comfortable in the white Methodist church and gradually establish their own congregations. Over time, then, cultural relationships between church and community can shift dramatically. As they shift, so do the ways in which power operates.

> **6.** Every pastoral situation consists of a "cultural flow,"
> comprised both of features common to other similar
> situations and of features distinctive to that one situation.

No one can be effective with power of any kind unless they understand how it functions. One of the central concepts in this chapter is that of cultural flow. This term refers to the many ways that various streams of culture meet and mix. We will look at these various streams and acknowledge that their meeting and mixing does not always go smoothly. We also will discuss one of the common dangers to a pastor moving from one pastoral setting to another: that of presuming too many similarities between them. Cultural tools help pastors learn to distinguish between the similarities and the contrasts, thus reducing the likelihood of stepping on land mines that will hinder opportunities to engage power productively.[5]

> **7.** Pastors must be in touch with their own "cultural flow" in
> order to be able to read the cultural dynamics of any situation.

Before they can interact effectively with the power that exists in their ministry setting, pastors need to understand how they are affected by the idiosyncrasies of their own cultural experiences. In modern life, we have tended to think in terms of psychology, looking at our human experiences privately, individualistically, and introspectively. This modern inclination has left us less aware of how our personal formation derives from social characteristics. We developed values and deep beliefs as we interacted with family, friends, schooling, community, etc. The wider and more diverse our social experience, the more complex and "peculiar to us" becomes our cultural heritage. The more awareness a pastor possesses about his or her own cultural baggage—this idiosyncratic cultural flow that he or she carries—the better able the pastor is to assess the cultural setting in which he or she finds himself/herself. Such a self-assessment is essential to dealing with power.

8. Often a power contest centers around whether one of the church's oldest and dearest deep beliefs is negotiable and could be replaced.

As we will see, culture is driven by elements that are not readily evident. In this theoretical model, the development of conflict symbolizes a challenge to these submerged but powerful elements. On the surface, such a disagreement appears often to emerge from a difference of opinion between old-time members and newcomers. A cultural analysis of congregations provides a way to identify the ensuing power struggle in terms that move away from personality. Familiar elements of the church life symbolize deeper issues that become threatened by suggestions for even surface changes. Understanding this, pastors can learn to redefine power and participate in the solution process more productively. The challenge is to help the congregation navigate through the anxiety of this perceived threat to an outcome that will benefit the church—in the long run as well as the short term.[6]

9. Culture can and will change over time, which means that its power also will change.

What is perhaps most apparent about culture is its resilience. It serves as a group's or society's conserving mechanism, since no human community can survive without some level of stability. To this end, culture's various and particular elements function like anchors. Yet, as a community's circumstances change (whether very slowly or suddenly), those same elements that have been familiar and cherished eventually will become challenged. From the long view of history, this process is normal, but often it is painful for those of the generation in which the change is most noticeable. Some of this discomfort arises from the gradual realization that the people in control are losing their grip on things. Why and how this phenomenon occurs will be one of our topics below.

These several claims summarizing culture and power might feel familiar to you or might sound odd at points. I am guessing that some of them make more sense to you than others. Because I believe that we cannot foster lasting and helpful change unless we understand what we are doing, the claims stated above need to be supported. What follows in the next section, then, is a description of concepts that make these claims what they are. Again, you might recognize some while others seem new. Don't be discouraged; you are learning a new way of thinking about church.

Key Concepts of Culture

Every human community—regardless of size, location, longevity, ethnicity, or influence—creates, nurtures, and transmits culture. We cannot do otherwise. Culture is what we are as we exist together. Even our theology and our religion get clothed in culture, most often without our being aware of it. So it makes a lot of sense that those of us who are involved with churches, synagogues, and mosques would use culture as a lens for figuring out the complexity of what is going on within our communities of faith. Not only this, but culture as a tool also points us to integral relationships between our religious groups and their particular settings.

In previous publications, I have described and applied a number of concepts out of the broad discipline of cultural anthropology to the life of congregations.[7] For our purposes, I will introduce the concepts of cultural confluence, the swamp of culture, and cultural perceptions of power. These concepts will help us to appreciate the many invisible ways that culture functions as power. Our goal is to help pastors and other church folk recognize culture's subtlety—yet still be prepared to work with, instead of simply opposing, it. Let us begin by examining the depths of culture, using the swamp as another metaphor.

The Cultural Swamp

Culture, like beauty, is more than skin deep. If we pay attention only to the elements of a community that are the most obvious, we still won't get it. Both secular and religious writers in recent years have explored the deeper elements of culture, creating models to help identify these depths.[8] The primary metaphor for the book provides us with a way to speak of culture as a swamp, consisting of three layers.

Up on the shore. The first and most obvious layer of culture can be simply termed the "stuff." An object or practice of a group qualifies as some of its cultural stuff. If we were to study any group's or society's stuff, the lists generated would be long and elaborate. Buildings, decorations, furniture, mission statements, routines, ceremonies, etc., all constitute cultural stuff. The most evident stuff for a

The swamp of your church or community is bigger than you think.

congregation would include its physical plant, its sanctuary, its style of worship, its current membership, and so on. All of these items are easy to note since they are readily apparent. Every bit of the stuff emerges in the church's life over time, from its very beginning, as it seeks to do things that fulfill its goals. Just like a swamp's shoreline, cultural stuff is easy to spot.

In the water. What makes stuff tricky, though, is that its meaning is not as evident as its presence. Stuff is like the parts of the swamp that set on the shore: You can see them plainly, but if you don't recognize that there is a whole lot more *under* the water's surface, you will be in big trouble! Alligators who grow to adulthood know that what happens up on the shore of the swamp is only part of the story of swamp life. So let us think about the next layer of culture as that part that we see just under the water line, as if we were swimming in the water. This layer of culture consists of all the things that the members of the group say about the group in order to explain why the stuff is what it is. This second layer exists in that realm of water where the alligator (and other swamp creatures) is used to swimming from place to place. It is the culture's "sayings."

Imagine, for instance, that a visitor comes to your church on a Sunday morning and participates in worship. Afterward, she inquires of you what a certain symbol, piece of art, or ritual means, what it stands for. As a member of that church (and therefore, one who helps to bear its culture), you provide an answer that you have learned from your experience there. Your answer gives a certain interpretation to the object of the visitor's question. Your answer places a particular kind of value on the object or action, such as:

- "We sing praise music for a half-hour to thank God for our lives and to get ourselves ready to listen for the Word."
- "The black Jesus in the painting tells our congregation that God is not one color but made all colors of people, including us."
- "The Apostle's Creed unites us with Christians throughout the ages."
- "Our children's choir shows everyone who worships here that children are very important to us and that they contribute in essential ways to weekly worship."

Sayings like these seek to make sense out of all the group's or community's stuff. They are necessary, since a church's culture—like that of any other group or community—must have sense-making structures. To the longtime group member, the sayings seem to say it all. But to the astute newcomer or observer, there inevitably will be aspects of the stuff that the sayings do not seem to explain, or to explain well.

Consider, for instance, an experience that I once had when I preached one Sunday for a pastor who was on vacation. I never had been to this particular congregation before, which was in a small farm town about an hour away. When I arrived prior to worship, one or two persons greeted me and ushered me to the chancel area of the sanctuary. As I sat down and looked around, everyone there appeared very somber, with only an occasional whisper or movement. Even the few children sat still and hushed. The worship service felt heavy, as though the congregation was carrying a large weight that it did not know how to put down. I did not feel inspired! But I preached at the appointed time as well as I could and was glad when the time for the benediction arrived. After pronouncing words that I hoped would be encouraging, the organist began to play a postlude and people rose from their places in the pews. They began to smile— albeit weakly, it seemed to me—as they shook hands with each other and headed toward the fellowship hall not far from the sanctuary. "Well," I thought, "at least they are showing a little more energy."

No one came to greet me right after worship. No one attempted to catch my gaze and smile, nod or wave approvingly. No one offered to walk me to the fellowship hall. Because I was a visitor, I was curious to see how I would be treated in the informal setting of the coffee time, so I waited to see if anyone would acknowledge my presence. As I stood in the fellowship hall for about ten minutes—a long time to be alone in a crowd!—I mused on the sight that I was beholding. No glances, no waves, no greetings, no conversation, no hospitality! Finally, one person came to say hello. She was an older woman, retirement age, who shook my hand and told me her name. Then, in a moment that I never have forgotten in all these years, she exclaimed with gusto, "We're glad you're here; we're a warm and friendly church!" She followed that statement with a grin that split her face and crinkled her eyes.

In reply, I must have said something innocuous and polite. In my mind, however, the thought that shouted out was, "You sure could have fooled me!" Yet it was clear that this woman was very sincere in what she said. She believed in her bones that her congregation was a caring group of people. It probably was so, to those who had been members for years and had not alienated themselves from the others. But to this one-time visitor, this newcomer, this outsider, that woman's statement was totally contradicted by the behaviors that I was observing.

The outsider's feeling of hearing one thing and experiencing something very different offers a noteworthy clue to something more in that church's culture. Most of today's congregations have existed for many years and thus have developed a culture that is well-established. Longtime members typically don't think about their church's culture beyond the two layers that are more obvious, i.e., the stuff and the sayings.

Down in the mud. Yet if we continue with the swamp metaphor, we begin to realize that, indeed, there is much more to church culture than meets the eye. What gives the swamp the support that it needs to exist is its massive, dark section layer, hidden below the water's surface: the mud. Although this enormous portion of the cultural swamp is deeply submerged, it holds the keys to the swamp's very character. What is submerged are beliefs, deeply held, hardly ever spoken aloud, hardly ever thought about by anyone. These deepest beliefs took their place in the mud during the group's (think "church's") earlier years, as it learned from its experience what worked, what it could trust. Submerged parts of the culture do not see the light of day without some prompting. Most commonly, the prompting occurs when a new piece of stuff appears, one that does not seem to fit in with the other stuff. Then the swamp water begins to stir mightily, kicking up pieces of mud; at that point, the longtime members are beginning to feel upset! They will tend to focus on the stuff itself, not realizing that it is what is submerged down in the mud that ultimately is being threatened. Newcomers to the church, for their part, are bewildered by such a turn of events and can't understand why the old-timers are not persuaded by reason. Such is the tremendous but murky power of the submerged part of the cultural swamp.

In other words, culture itself is defined by this third and bottom layer, by what is in the mud, not by the two top layers of the swamp's ecology. Recognizing culture's essence at this almost mysterious dimension marks a significant shift away from popular perspectives on culture. Even though it takes time to get used to thinking of culture in this way, the swamp metaphor offers great potential. Not only will behavior in your congregation begin to make more sense, but you will discover ways of dealing with problems that work better. For one thing, you will begin to see how disagreements over decisions (e.g., "Should we allow hip-hop music in worship?" "Who has the right to a key to the church kitchen?" "What color should the pew cushions be?") actually represent differing submerged beliefs. In today's churches, these differing beliefs exist often, for example, between newcomers and longtime members, and between older and younger members. This is the case because the groups at odds with each other have differing life experiences that shape the submerged elements of their respective subcultures.[9] In part, the power that is at stake here derives from the strength of the cultural mud within the church's various subgroups.

Although some of a congregation's mud might be religious or theological in nature, much of it will not be so. That is, the religious claims that a church asserts operate more at the level of the sayings. Being suspended in the water, sayings are valuable to the church for what they represent about its aspirations, its sense of identity. By contrast, much of the mud in the church's cultural swamp represents deep beliefs that the church learned as it dealt with its real-life situations. Material in the mud is based on what was perceived in the church's earliest days to have worked well. It eventually comes to terms with its own notions of what is real, what is true, how time is construed, what space is like, what humans are like, and how we are to get along with each other.[10] Some of these categories can involve religious dimensions, while others do not require them.

Another characteristic of a church's cultural mud is that it is not necessarily good or bad. It is, in important respects, simply what it is. Let us repeat an important point once more: The various pieces exist in the congregation as a result of ways in which that body of believers perceived certain of their experiences together to turn out the way that they did. Initially, many (but probably not all) of the submerged pieces are positive or helpful. This makes them powerful to the church in a constructive manner. As the years go by, circumstances that gave rise to those submerged pieces could change, thereby changing the dynamics within which any one of them might continue to be useful in the same way. Analyzing the power of submerged beliefs begins by suspending judgment on their goodness or badness.

Understanding the characteristics and role of a church's cultural mud is a major key to power. We will look, then, at some examples of statements that represent the kind of submerged beliefs that a congregation might discover as it searches deep within its own swamp. Illustrations are beneficial here because it is easy at first to confuse what is in the water with what is down in the mud. In other words, sayings must be distinguished from what is deeper, what is submerged. The actual wording that becomes used to express this layer of culture will vary by church. The point here is that this bottom layer does exist and that it is full of fundamental meaning. Also, we will see in the next section that the submerged parts derive from sources outside the congregation as well as from within it. Regardless of source, submerged swamp material is hard to discern initially. Neither the outsider nor the insider can be comfortably confident about these deepest elements. For this reason, this challenging discovery process is even more critical since our eventual goal is information that is accurate.[11]

Alligators who know their way around the swamp realize that the mud at the bottom can be tricky or dangerous if you do not know what is there. Once clear and interpreted, the submerged mud pieces point to the power dynamics in the congregation. Churches seeking to navigate more wisely through the swamp of their ministry field need to uncover their own submerged beliefs. Some of them might sound like these:

- "Truth is welcome from any source, as long as it does not contradict our interpretation of the Bible."

This kind of submerged belief is related directly to the congregation's religious orientation. It suggests a more conservative, traditional view of the nature of truth. It recognizes that life in our world today draws knowledge from many directions, but it wants to affirm an anchoring quality for one religious source in particular. The challenge for a submerged belief like this one is in acknowledging that the Bible can be interpreted in many ways. If this congregation limits truth to its own filter, it might miss something that would help it grow in its own Christian witness. Yet, the belief became part of the church's mud because it was perceived, at some point in the congregation's life, to work, to help that church solve some of its typical problems.

- "Being together gives us our best opportunity to live as we prefer and affirm our own dignity in the world."

Some churches arise out of communities that have been marginalized by the wider society. Most ethnic groups in the United States have endured some degree of oppression (Irish, African, Italian, Japanese, native tribes, etc.), and their places of worship will reflect this experience. It would be expected that church, then, becomes a haven of identity, expression, and affirmation of each group's practices and values. To an observer, some of these values and practices might appear to be holding onto the past or even threatening to "the American way of life." Regardless of the opinions of outsiders, submerged pieces like this one will exist within the cultural mud of congregations with an ethnic background of some form of subjugation.

- "Starting and ending on time honors the busy lives of those who participate in our activities."

Modern Western societies have become very time-conscious. With the advent of industrial efficiency at the end of the nineteenth century, increasing numbers of American institutions have come to measure time discretely and sequentially. We have become accustomed to doing "this" for so long before we do "that" next for a certain length of time, and so on. This submerged piece of the wider American society has found its way into many churches as well. Worship is to begin promptly at 11:00 A.M. and conclude no later than noon. Some congregations might even discover a submerged piece that says "Punctuality is next to godliness," assuming without question that there must be a verse in the Bible that supports this belief. By contrast, African American Christian traditions often operate with a conscious awareness that they are not bound by a clock. For most of the world until the technology of widespread timepieces, activities began and ended by opportunity rather than measurement.

- "Newcomers might become insiders after years of proving their diligence and loyalty to what already is in place."

This kind of submerged piece strikes me as emerging (then becoming stuck in the mud) in a second or later generation of a congregation's life. Many of us have experience in congregations where visitors and new members feel welcomed, but only to a point. Once a congregation feels that it can survive indefinitely, it sticks some submerged pieces about privilege into the bottom of its mud. One of the reasons that such a church would have survived up to that point is through faithful efforts of trusted persons. A submerged belief that echoes such experiences can be helpful later; however, it also could work against the inclusion of new folks whose energy and insight are necessary for the next chapter of the church's life.

- "The most desirable parts of the facilities and space are controlled by those with the most status."

Status is a phenomenon that all of us experience in the various contexts of our daily lives. We know that particular persons, as well as certain organizational or community positions, come to be regarded with special recognition and deference. Churches are not immune to this human social tendency.[12] As a consequence, persons in churches often become "rewarded" in unofficial ways, sometimes by the power to use and manage valuable church space. This can and does occur even in denominations that designate specific requirements of rule and property to certain offices. In these traditions, new pastors especially can be unpleasantly surprised and tripped up if they do not recognize ahead of time the power that can accrue to status and space.

These are five examples of what submerged pieces within a church's cultural mud could look like. They suggest that thinking of culture in terms of a swamp can be most instructive (perhaps even in a healthy, humorous way). This swamp analogy, with its three layers, presses us to move beyond simple or conventional views of culture, church, and power. As the stories and examples imply, it can help us to see and do things differently.

Yet, the swamp does not tell us enough about what makes culture and power so complicated. In order to begin to understand, for instance, why newcomers and longtime members of a church might not see eye to eye on everything, we need to borrow yet another water-related metaphor from nature. This metaphor perhaps is not as colorful as the swamp, yet it opens up a world of insight that we often struggle to articulate. Our second metaphor is that of *confluence*, a series of little rivulets, streams, and rivers that join together along their eventual journey to an ocean. What happens to the water from each source—whether large or small, deep or shallow—as two or more of the flowing bodies meet each other? Do we find logjams or smooth sailing? If we pay closer attention to each of these cultural streams, we can learn to anticipate the answer to this question for any context to which it is applied.

Culture as Confluence (Streams)

As a boy, I remember visiting the mountains and ocean beaches not far from where I grew up. Around forty-five inches of rain per year fall in Oregon's Willamette Valley, so there was plenty of water visible around me in any direction. The Rickreall Creek emerges on the east side of the Coast Range mountains, flowing away from the Pacific Ocean, down the thick, green, steep hills into my home town, and then further east until it meets the Willamette River at Salem. For its part, the Willamette River flows south to north, from below Eugene through the fertile valley that bears its name. About 100 miles later, the Willamette—which has grown in size and depth—meets one of the largest rivers in North America, the Columbia, at Oregon's largest city, Portland. The sheer size of their meeting is a phenomenon that few Americans have witnessed—aside from the Mississippi River and Niagara Falls. Waters in the Columbia River are deep, fast, and dangerous to swimmers and small boats. Those waters carry all the way from remote parts of Canada and the Rocky Mountains, hundreds of miles east and north. For ninety miles past Portland, the Columbia moves majestically north and west. Finally, the mighty river spreads out like a fan as it spills tens of thousands of gallons of water per minute into the Pacific Ocean. Columbia's mouth is so wide that a bridge across it was impossible to construct until recent years.

Such is a snapshot of one of North America's most extensive natural drainage networks. It can be staggering to realize that every drop of that water enters the journey at some earlier point where many of the streams are smaller than the ones that they enter. Ecologists refer to the place where these waters meet as a point of "confluence," or "flowing with." When the smaller streams meet the mightier ones, it appears at first glance that the larger stream always "wins"; that is, its water and speed swallows up the smaller stream. Yet, consider that everything borne by the smaller stream when it entered the larger one ends up in the larger stream. What happens to those elements from there is anyone's guess and depends upon circumstances downstream.

What I have described here is a generalized but accurate explanation of a readily observable phenomenon in nature. It also can be used as an analogy for culture. Like streams of water, culture also involves streams that emerge and flow from specific sources into larger bodies. By learning to notice the presence of all of the streams, we are better equipped to understand the culture that we face at any particular point in which we enter the flowing water. In the context of the United States, these streams can be categorized in about five ways. We will meet them one by one, from the largest to the smallest. As we do so, keep in mind that each one of these streams of culture also has swamps floating in it. In other words, once we recognize the presence of a particular stream, we could analyze its depths all the way down to its submerged material. In combining the models from both of these metaphors, we begin to become aware of how intricate and even confusing culture can be. It should come as no surprise, then, that we sometimes are caught off-guard by the ways in which power appears out of cultural dynamics that we do not yet understand.

Macroculture. When we think about life in the United States, we quickly can identify certain elements that are fairly in common. These characteristics have a power of their own, regardless of whether we recognize them, understand them, practice them, or even like them. They constitute what I call American "macroculture," that largest-scale stream of culture that people in the U.S.A. encounter. Some of the most traditional and commonly recognized stuff of this macroculture include the Declaration of Independence, Washington, D.C., the song "America, the Beautiful," baseball, the Civil War, Thanksgiving Day, and so on. In the wake of the terrorist attacks on Manhattan and the Pentagon, the Twin Towers that were destroyed also have become for many a symbol of the United States

One particular episode during the September 11th coverage demonstrated so clearly to me the power and effects of American macroculture. A network television reporter was roaming the streets of Manhattan and stopped to talk to three New York City firefighters clearing some of the extensive rubble along the streets. In this case, all three firefighters were people of color; their surnames were difficult to pronounce, and at least one of them spoke with an obvious accent. Clearly, here were three young adults whose families had immigrated to the United States not too many years earlier and not from Western Europe. As they were interviewed briefly one by one, I had not expected to hear what they said. Each one of them, in their own way, said that they loved their country, that America is strong, that it will survive these horrible attacks, and that they were proud to be Americans.

It would be difficult to find a more dramatic illustration of how macroculture works. Out of families born in non-Western nations, these three dedicated firefighters clearly identified in a time of great crisis with their adopted homeland. To be sure, they continue to identify with their own ethnic heritages, with all the distinctions and richness that each one over many centuries has developed. Nothing that the firefighters said denied the importance of those heritages. In time of national crisis, however, these three men expressed a deep loyalty to the larger cultural world in which they now live. For them, being American is a part of their identity. They have learned enough about American macroculture to embrace and promote at least certain aspects of it.

Mesocultures. Being American, however, is defined not merely by large-scale features. Americans have a number of other characteristics that distinguish them from each other, which operate on a smaller scale. These characteristics are borne by the waters of several streams that function in between national and local levels. They are in the middle levels, hence called mesocultures. We can arrange them according to region, class, gender, orality, generation, and race/ethnicity.

Regional. Among the common language used in the United States are references to distinct geographical areas of the country. Terms like "Northeast," "Deep South," "Midwest," and "West" denote not only different locations on a U.S. map; they also are recognized, if only vaguely, as designating difference in particular social and cultural practices. I became most conscious of these differences when I moved some years ago from Oregon to Illinois. Up to that point, I had spent years of my life in the Willamette Valley of Oregon, in the Puget Sound area of Washington State, near Los Angeles (which Mike Royko, a popular Chicago columnist during his lifetime, is reported to have called "the largest outdoor insane asylum in the world"), near Denver, and in southern Oregon (very rural). I had traveled little otherwise, except for one month-long study tour of western Europe as a high school student and a brief trip to the Washington, D.C., area.

So, although I had traveled in several states and countries, the brevity of these visits had not yet impressed upon me the significance of cultural difference. All of that ignorance began to change in my move to Illinois. The point is not that there is something about Illinois that is inherently inferior or faulty but that, from my unconscious cultural perspective, it was different, confusing, and at times troubling. For one thing, I had spent all of my life until then in view of mountains that provided orientation to direction. By contrast, Illinois is the sixth flattest state in the Union, so at first I could not figure out how to tell where I was going. Coming from a state with lots of lumber, I was used to frame houses; Illinois's housing stock appears to me mostly brick and stone, materials that I like very much. I had grown up in a state that continues to rank with the second-lowest ratio of church attendance in the nation. Illinois had more Roman Catholic and Lutheran churches than I ever had seen before.

Regional differences like these, however, can be minor compared to daily practices (stuff), statements of what is important (sayings), and deeper dimensions (submerged) underlying each of these regions. That is, cultural swamps exist also at the middle level of United States society. They reflect the distinctive experiences of the communities that settled, lived, established businesses, built churches, raised children, started schools, set up hierarchies of status and discrimination, etc., in those places. As I discovered over time, life in the Midwest does differ from life in the West in some observable and not-so-observable ways. Such differences, I could argue, also contribute to differences in the way that power appears and is used.[13] One American mesocultural category, then, represents the geographical regions and their distinctive cultural qualities.

Class. When I reflect upon my experience of growing up where I did, I also become aware of another mesocultural stream in my hometown. This one was a stream that was evident as I became aware of certain differences between the farm kids and the town kids, or between families whose fathers worked at the mill and those who owned businesses, taught school, or otherwise wore a shirt and tie to work. Level of income is not the only factor at play here: One of my friend's fathers was a truck driver and made half again what my father made teaching school. Yet there has developed in American society some observable relationships between income (economic), education (intellectual), and status (social). The noticeable variations between such relationships often are referred to as class differences. We commonly employ three categories to identify them: upper, middle, and lower.[14] To distinguish the complexity of this cultural stream even further, we are familiar with the use of a fourth category, working class.

To some, these categories might sound essentially economic and have nothing to do with culture. As we ruminate upon our own observations of social activity, however, we will grant that there is more involved in class than money. The 1960s television series, "The Beverly Hillbillies," ran on the premise of an impoverished Appalachian family who accidentally discovers oil on their property and moves to a posh Los Angeles community to enjoy "the good life." Most of the comedy in this series revolves around the newly rich Clampett family as it blissfully maintains quaint "down home" ways. Their habits and practices changed little, but more significantly, their deeper beliefs and values remained relatively intact, in spite of pressures to conform to the life of the elite. It is readily apparent in reruns of "The Beverly Hillbillies" that the tremendous financial windfall of the Clampetts did not significantly affect their culture.

So to what class did they belong? The world of television programming allows us to imagine a family whose economic standing and cultural preferences did not match common expectations. The fact that this series ran as a comedy suggests a common understanding in American society that cultural swamps do indeed exist for class. Alligators who are raised in one class of swamp find navigating in swamps of other classes difficult, no matter which direction "up" or "down" the class ladder one might end up traveling. One cannot have power if one is not able to understand and accept all the layers of the cultural swamp that confronts them.

Gender. We have seen already that women in society generally have a harder time than men in defining self and power (see Chapter 2). As we reflect on this phenomenon honestly, we begin to realize that it is pervasive, cutting across virtually all other social distinctions. In other words, it hardly seems to matter whether the women in question live in the U.S.A. or Indonesia, are black, brown, yellow, or white, have a Ph.D. or no schooling at all, or live in a mansion or a straw hut, human social groupings almost universally distinguish roles and power by gender, and women end up on the short end of the stick.

On the basis of this general observation, it is fair to say that gender constitutes another stream of mesoculture. While the details may vary, the distinction remains quite consistent. Practices (stuff), proverbs (sayings), and unspoken beliefs (submerged) in the cultural muds of virtually all human communities indicate that females and males are treated differently.

As we know, these differences have translated until very recent times into a preferential position for men and a secondary, often subservient position for women. That those differences still persist even in postmodern America suggests the pervasive and long-standing assumptions that are at stake. Gender surely functions as a stream of middle-level culture in the United States. It would be grossly naïve to suppose that the cultural dynamics of gender do not affect the church.

Race/ethnicity. Perhaps it is easier for many readers to recognize the cultural distinctiveness present between the many racial and ethnic groups now existing in the United States. These many streams of culture function at the middle level because, in most cases, they are not limited to geographical boundaries. People of native, African, Asian, Latin, and other ethnic backgrounds live virtually everywhere in the United States. To differing degrees, they understand and participate in various elements of American macroculture while maintaining aspects of their culture of origin.

Today's public American arena has become much more sensitized to the severe and protracted effects of racial/ethnic oppression and injustice. A cultural interpretation of racial discrimination would focus upon the efforts of the macroculture to limit or reduce the effects of racial/ethnic swamps upon the wider society. Avid supporters of macroculture have created over the decades logjams at the confluence where it meets racial/ethnic streams of culture. Logjams have the effect of preserving extant forms of power and actively discouraging the inclusion of those from other sources. When alligators are in the wrong swamp, the power that they knew in the home swamp probably will not work!

Orality. A less-recognized but widely dispersed and pervasive category of American mesoculture exists in many places and in many forms. It is a category evident among many racial and ethnic groups and in Euro-American communities as well. Its primary features revolve around localized, extended-family-type relationships and upon the power of the spoken word. "Traditional oral culture" is found in rural areas, small towns and in working-class urban neighborhoods.[15] In the social groups that function with orality, everyone knows everyone else, warts and all. Their valued knowledge is based upon the group's history and traditions and not upon expert, specialized learning. Wisdom for living that arises from the culture's brand of knowledge becomes transmitted and affirmed through the telling of stories and the quoting of proverbial sayings. Conventional farming, mill and factory work, domestic and day labor all typify the kinds of hands-on occupations prominent in oral cultures. Discussing job choice in this way for oral culture is misleading, however: A job is a means to an end, that end being to value and preserve inherited practices and customs through gatherings, storytelling, and wisdom conveyed through proverbs.

This general summary of oral cultures might seem too abstract until one begins to recall childhood memories of family gatherings at holiday times. After dinner, as the children run and play, the older adults sit in the best chairs and recall incidents and events. Every extended family seems to have at least one colorful storyteller, a man or woman whose recounting of humorous or poignant moments in the life of the clan remind and affirm listeners of what they know to be right and good. Family reunions abound with such experiences. In fact, the case could be made that most of us grew up in families in which streams of oral culture were evident, if not often, at least at special occasions. Many of us with college and graduate degrees seek throughout our lifetimes to disengage from our oral culture roots out of embarrassment, as though it were an inferior way of life.

Wise alligators realize that oral culture remains a strong feature in many American swamps. It is not a problem to be remedied but a culture to respect on its own terms. It creates and uses its own forms of power, even when those forms often appear to those who use them as impotent before the never-ending onslaught of postmodern technology, big government, and multinational business interests. Pastors in rural or small-town churches must honor the forms of oral culture that they encounter if they are to develop enough power to do significant ministry there.[16]

Generations. Last but not least, American society is laced with several forms of middle-level culture are based upon certain age groupings. Generational theorists arrange American generations by approximately twenty-year spans and argue that certain events and experiences affect the generations in their particular ways.[17] For instance, my parents' generation was raised during the Great Depression and World War II. Economic deprivation as children and worldwide military victory as young adults shaped this generation's view of life very deeply. Their children, baby boomers, grew up witnessing the assassinations of President Kennedy and Dr. Martin Luther King, Jr., as well as the ethical and political ambiguity of the Vietnam military conflict. These events, by contrast, had little shaping influence upon the next generation, often called "Xers." Instead, they are products of MTV and the HIV/AIDS epidemic.

Generational cultures exist in these and all generational groups.

They account for some of the political distress in the United States and quite a bit of conflict in American churches. While much of the popular literature on these generational differences might appear shallow and trendy, it is based upon a phenomenon that would be difficult to refute. Cultural swamps are formed in each generation. Their lowest parts, the submerged beliefs, bump into each other, sometimes with great distress.

Here, then, are six categories designed to reveal more of the complexity of living in American society. Generational, oral cultural, gender, racial/ethnic, class and regional mesocultures flow throughout the United States in combinations that gradually become familiar and then unexpectedly change. Whether the swamps in all these mesocultures flow together smoothly or jam up is a question of empirical study. However, much of our own experiences would suggest that jams occur and are not easy to negotiate. It is at the point of swamp floods that we become especially aware of culture's power. Since we live out our daily lives in specific, local contexts, the prospect of swamp floods multiplies. We have spoken so far of macro- and mesocultures, located on the larger end of the scale. There also are smaller scales of culture that go into the intricate mix that constitutes our cultural experience.

Microculture. The broadest of smaller-scale cultural categories describes an identifiable area, such as a small town, a city and/or its neighborhoods, or a rural county, in which a localized culture exists. These micro (i.e., small) cultures represent where any one of us actually lives in its particularity. All of the larger streams of culture—macro- and the various meso-streams—influence us at the level of the microculture. What makes microcultures so interesting is that they are idiosyncratic. As the larger streams flow through your town, they interact with the history and culture of the community. This process over time creates the stuff, the sayings, and the submerged pieces that constitute the swamp of microculture for your town. Hence, microcultures can and do have some swamp materials in common. However, because of the particular and localized nature of each town, city, or neighborhood, every microculture is distinct. One might look just the same as another, but it will not share every single submerged piece with that lookalike.

I learned this lesson the hard way early in my pastoral career. My second parish call was to a 100-member church in a small town back in my home state. I was eager to show the congregation how effective I could be because I thought that I knew what I was getting into. After all, this was a small town and I had grown up in one, so I figured that I knew how I would be received by the church and town. It was a church of my denomination, so I figured that it would do things in the way that I had learned our form of government to function. I was mistaken on all counts. While my home town had been steadily growing throughout my lifetime, my new church's town had lost over two-thirds of its residents. The disappearing economic base there had cast a quiet pall over an otherwise bucolic-looking community. I also discovered that town residents were very independent and private. They did not open up to newcomers well, even when I made myself available in community activities. With respect to the congregation itself, it had roots to 1859 but had merged twice with churches of other denominations. Although Presbyterian in name and affiliation, the church included many older members who still considered themselves one of the other three denominations. They went along with Presbyterian polity grudgingly and as sparingly as possible. A church situation that I thought I had interpreted ahead of time turned out to be different, in difficult ways, than I had realized.

Unfortunately, this experience of mine could be a mirror for many other pastors who, over the course of a pastoral career, move from one community to another. I had assumed erroneously that similarities between the tops of two microcultural swamps represented the same kind of congruence at their bottoms. As I listen to seminary students and other pastors talk, it is easy for them to arrive at this same incorrect conclusion. To summarize this discussion on microculture: First, it is the local stream that always has its own idiosyncratic nature. Second, microculture becomes one complex but useful lens for understanding the challenges of pastors entering the world of a given parish. Wise alligators know that certain parts of the swamp might look the same above the water, but it is what is down far below the surface that counts.

Organizational. Culture has yet two more small-scale streams. Both of them reside within the groups and organizations that we humans create because we are a highly associational species. Organizations themselves create, nurture, and transmit their own cultures, which—as we can see by now—are deeply affected by the larger-scale streams of culture that flow around and through them. We can speak, hence, first of the culture of the organization. Secondly, we can speak of the culture of the organization at specific points along its lifecycle as its "ethos." These are more subtle but still very strong elements of any swamp. They are cultural streams that the bull alligators know best and have used in their exercise of power. Let us consider them briefly.

Organizational culture is a more minute version of microculture. It bears its own particular handling of the streams that have impinged upon it from macroculture, the several mesocultures, and the organization's immediate microculture. For our purposes, this means that the swamp refers not only to the congregation itself but also to the church's microculture (and how the latter has been influenced by the larger streams beyond it). Perhaps this point now is obvious. However, I have been amazed over the years as a pastor how I ignored these connections—and suffered for it. I continue to be aware of how frequently pastors (and seminary students) seem to prefer to downplay the cultural realities of their congregations and those of their congregations' microcultures. Remember, each one has built its own swamp, and (pardon the repetition of metaphors) when you have that many swamps showing up in the swamp, something is bound to happen!

To summarize, then, all the formal elements that constitute cultural streams on the larger scales also exist to create the culture of your church. It is neither completely the same, nor completely different, than the church's microculture. Your corner of the swamp has currents that flow out of other corners of the swamp. Alligators who know how to ride those currents are in a better position to utilize power.

Ethos. It might seem as though there could be no further scale for measuring culture, but let me offer one more. Like other phenomena created with life, our human organizations are not static; they do not stand still. Even when appearing to coast along, churches experience momentum that actually affects the dynamics of their culture. A growing number of writers, both secular and religious, now recognize that churches, along with other organizations, go through predictable stages.[18] This lifecycle spans across the organization's founding, its jittery growth periods, its survival and establishment, its leveling off and almost inevitable decline, and its desperate years and possible death. The cultural flavor of each stage or phase is palpably different from the others, and it is predictable, too. If we compared a church in one stage with a business or other kind of organization in the same stage, we would notice similarities. These similarities have little to do with content but everything to do with fundamental organizational matters, such as flexibility and control, attitude toward outsiders and insiders, clarity of vision, the nature of performance, and so on.[19] Thus, the culture of each of these respective organizational stages can be termed the ethos of that stage.

One of the implications of this notion of church ethos has to do with power. There is more willingness in a young organization to try new things, especially when compared with a church that is over a century old and has been doing the same things for years as the neighborhood changes around it. The culture of flexibility is very different from that of repetition. This means that the power at stake in how decisions get made and carried out will function very differently. Power in a culture of repetition feels comfortable to insiders and stifling to newcomers. It is as though the swamp's flow of fresh water has become constricted. By contrast, the power of new churches often is energizing, as fresh as the air and water in the swamp after a huge rainstorm. Wise alligators know the difference and realize that stagnation eventually hurts all life in the swamp.

Confluence and Power

In the previous section, I have outlined a theory of culture that I call confluence. Its structure and terminology seek to help us make sense out of the intricate and often puzzling customs by which we experience human life around us. Combined with the swamp metaphor, confluence attempts not to impose a framework but to reveal what we actually encounter, in all of its multifarious characteristics. Certainly some local contexts are more complicated than others, but all we have to do is read the daily newspaper to acknowledge that the big world out there is not so far away. Being able to recognize the cultural dynamics of a given situation offers us the chance to see both the swamp and its alligators with greater clarity. In so doing, we are in a better position to determine both the nature and location of power as well as to decide on our place in the swamp. The less that we take for granted, the better prepared we can be to engage power for benefit.

Culture and Power:

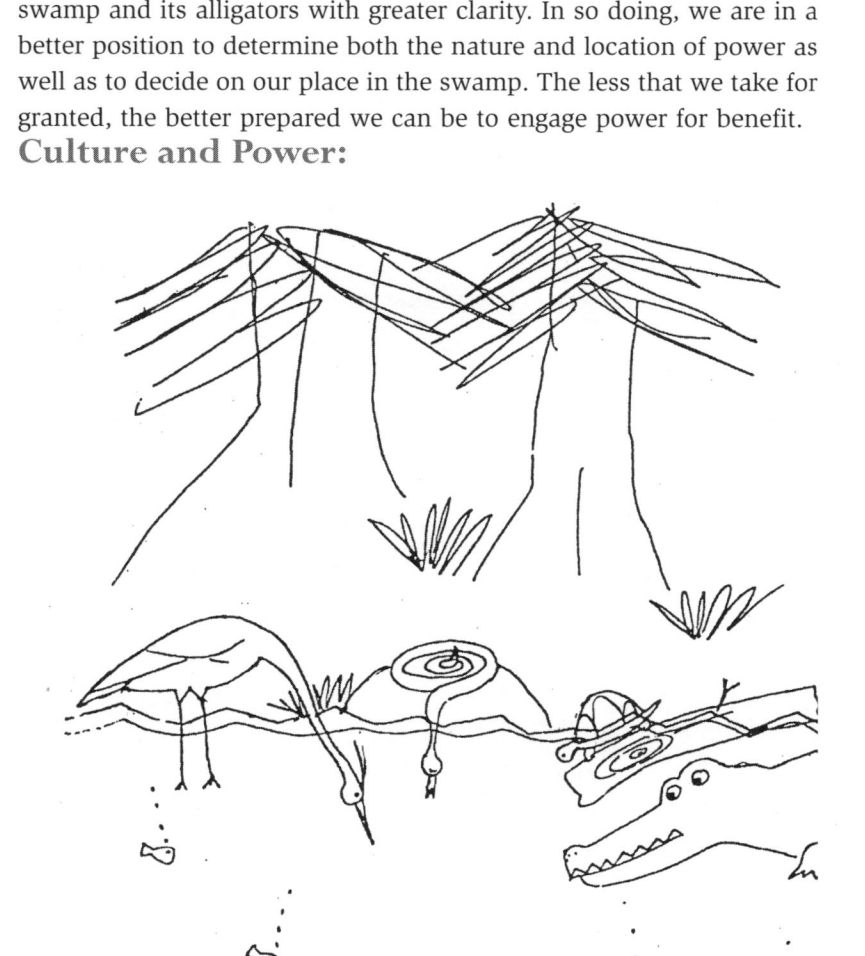

Can anybody tell what's down here?

An Illustration with Religion

Trying to understand relationships between church, culture, and power is not new.[20] What perhaps makes the subject of this chapter distinctive is the relatively new emphasis upon treating the theme in terms of the social sciences. Religious people are fairly at ease using religious language but often do not know how to incorporate other perspectives, fearing that the latter will take over the conversation. Christians need to learn how to maintain these other perspectives in a creative tension.

Perceptions of Power

Eric Law's work demonstrates that such creative tension can be very productive. In his first book, *The Wolf Shall Dwell with the Lamb,* Rev. Law is concerned primarily with power in the church and its cultural dimensions. His interdisciplinary framing of racial dynamics in the United States provides a ready application of the redemptive value of understanding power through the lens of culture. Law engages this creative methodology as a result of his own background. He was born in Hong Kong to Chinese Christian parents and moved to the United States when he was fourteen.[21] His experiences as a person of color in a mostly white American denomination have helped him to approach matters of race in a fresh way. As a result, his biblical interpretation and theological insights are novel and profound.

Initially, Rev. Law wanted to understand why he himself—and others—felt confusion and anger over certain processes and interactions that took place in both denominational and ecumenical gatherings of Christians. Over time, Law became aware of cultural differences based out of his own life, between Hong Kong and "the dominant culture of the United States."[22] This dominant culture, Law argues, is shaped by values of the educated, middle- and upper-class white elements of U.S. society. As increasing numbers of persons immigrate to the United States from non-European countries, those dominant values become implicitly challenged by other values imported along with the new immigrants. Deep beliefs, such as the equality of every person, are not universally shared among world cultures. Law began to realize that his own frustration about feeling powerless in the United States was directly related to cultural differences between his home and his adopted land.[23]

Law's interest in understanding culture and power led him to resources from cultural anthropology. Based largely upon his experience of participating in multicultural gatherings of Christians, he began to formulate his thinking about what he calls "perceptions of power."[24] He noticed that people from countries that are more economically and socially hierarchical are less likely to believe that they have power. By contrast, those with origins in many Western European and British Commonwealth nations tend to behave as though they do have power as well as a right to exercise it.[25] These two categories of perceiving one's own power tend to run along racial lines: the latter are whites, the former are people of color. Regardless of whether all the persons in a gathering are Christian, people of color usually feel dominated by the whites. Law says that this is because of cultural differences rather than theological ones. White "solutions" to recognizing the disparity in perception often do not work, Law argues, because they are based on premises from white culture. He believes, however, that it is possible to overcome these power disparities with greater dignity to all. He then develops a strategy about the sharing of power, one that he frames in terms both of anthropology and by Christian theology.[26]

Interpreting with "Confluence"

Rather than focusing upon the particular solution that Law offers, let us instead seek to understand how that solution demonstrates insightful use of cultural concepts. In terms from this chapter, Law's observations about multicultural church gatherings exemplify logjams between racial/ethnic mesocultures and American macroculture. Indeed, mesocultural streams will carry some differing beliefs at the bottoms of their own swamps. Because the macroculture dominates, however, those who are most embedded in it have a harder time realizing that newer arrivals to the United States might not understand or accept what is at the bottom of this larger swamp. Power tends to accrue to the cultural stream that dominates: A brook that empties into a large river sees its contents swallowed up. Human communities do not like to be swallowed up. In the midst of power that they must face all around them, groups seek ways to exercise power that they know already. They are like a new family of alligators that gets dumped into an unfamiliar swamp where other alligators already live. In the new context, there will be considerable negotiating to undertake in order to navigate well.

Confluence and the Individual

Law's approach to multicultural analysis also helps us to realize something else. It is, as we noted first in chapter two, that power derives not simply from individuals but perhaps even more significantly out of the group. This insight tends to fly in the face of American individualism, but nonetheless it is a point worth pondering. What particular persons do, and what communities promote, tolerate, and condemn, is directly related to that community's swamp. More specifically, individual action is heavily influenced by the swamp's submerged pieces rather than the stuff or even the sayings. The swamp's stuff and sayings are what they are because the community perceives them to express the submerged level, not the other way around. In other words, individual behavior is judged by the community's understanding of its own deeper cultural dimensions. This particular insight helps to explain why American society is so divided in the present generation over many social issues: There is not agreement on all the submerged pieces of the swamp.

One of my experiences on a recent teaching trip to Kenya can illustrate this point about individuals, group, and power. Before we left, my wife and I read in a travel guide that petty street crime in Kenya many times was handled by the crowds. If it catches the suspected thief, a crowd might beat him to death. We commented to each other about the apparent brutality of such an action and wondered if it actually still occurred. We found out the answer firsthand during a travel day. Having just brought us into a city, our driver maneuvered the car onto a downtown street, parking by the curb for a few minutes. We got out of the car to stretch, since we had been sitting for a long time. Before we realized what was happening, several people ran by us, on the sidewalk and on the street, gathering about a half-block away. We turned our attention to the small, tight crowd down the street. A woman on the sidewalk noticed our curiosity. In a matter-of-fact voice, she said to us, "That man snatched a purse in the store and tried to get away. They probably will kill him."

Beverly and I looked at each other in silence. A swirl of thoughts ran through my mind. As complete strangers, in a country and culture that is not ours, we stood virtually no chance of stopping the man's beating. This punishment seemed too harsh, yet we must admit that we do not understand much about life in Kenya. As our car pulled away onto the street, we passed by the tight crowd and craned our necks to see. I felt helpless and guilty, as I wondered if the man would survive.

The power to which any one person might have access is related to their perceived position in the cultural confluence of the context in question. A student in one of my classes made this point humorously but accurately one day when Eric Law himself was a guest in class. At one point, Law was demonstrating how to do power analysis. He would invite different pairs of students to stand up and then ask the class which one of the two normally would be perceived as having more power. After a few illustrations with students, Rev. Law asked me to stand up, along with one of the young men in the class. I am culturally Euro-American and serve on the faculty of an African American theological school. So when Rev. Law asked the class which one of us was perceived as having more power, the class responded with "Dr. Thompson." Without missing a beat, the student standing up with me replied with a grin, "Unless we're in the 'hood!" Everyone in class laughed! His point was right on target. Power and its perception hinges largely upon the specific situation, and that situation will be undergirded by the submerged cultural material of that immediate community. In other words, alligators learn to pay attention to where they are in the swamp; they know what they can and cannot do, when and how.

Maps and Compass:
Pastoral Ministry as the Power of Culture

My primary aim in this chapter is to introduce a cultural framework, a theory that will help pastors become wise alligators in the swamps of ministry. As preceding sections have maintained, these swamps are constituted in part by streams of water running into the one swamp. I trust that all these metaphors are clear enough for the reader to understand the interpretive framework that they represent. It remains, then, to speak a little more explicitly about how such a cultural model can help pastors and churches with power. Let us consider a few general observations before moving to a list of action themes.

So many different creatures to take care of.

Confluence and Your Church

One of the insights to clarify from this chapter has to do with the sometimes subtle relationships between your congregation and the world around it. As a pastor, I have heard church members over the years talk about their church as though it were an island unto itself, literally and figuratively. I have to confess that, for many years, my pastoral mindset was similar. Even though I often learned more about the church's community than many of the members knew, I still did not think about the connections. With a cultural framework such as the one presented here, the connections can become much more evident. In other words, much of what is in the mud of the congregation's swamp originates from one of the larger cultural streams. A local church or parish is not created out of nothing; its initial cultural layers derive from the founding pastor, the ethnic group, the town or neighborhood and the particular denominational tradition.

It is too often the case, however, that the congregation ignores many of these streams, even as they are helping to make the congregation what it becomes. Consequently, the congregation is less able to be aware of how it deals with power. It will not be prepared to reflect upon its own practices (which are part of its cultural stuff) in order to dig down into its mud and reveal the submerged pieces that support its swamp. As Eric Law's observations in *The Wolf Shall Dwell* imply, these submerged elements will and do vary from one ethnic group to another, and—thus by logical extension—from one congregation to another. The clearer that a congregation can be about its cultural ties to the world around it, the better it will be able to discern its modes and means of power.

The Task of Theologizing

Some readers might be wondering at this point if a cultural approach to church and power leaves any room for theology. If a framework like this explains so much, what happens to the church's typical understanding of the normative role of thinking about the world from a divine perspective? The answer to this question at first might appear dismissive, as though religious reflection is being taken down a few notches. I believe that the opposite is true—that by locating theology's place in human experience, it will be better equipped to provide clarity rather than add to our human inclination to pride and confusion (see Genesis 11:1–9).

More specifically, it is helpful in this culture model to locate religious assertion and its theological reflection in the second layer of the cultural swamp. Culturally, theology is not in the swamp's mud; any theology rests upon philosophical assumptions that emerge from it. One simple way to illustrate this point is to compare three congregations with comparable theological claims but different ethnic backgrounds. It is not difficult to identify a Korean American, an African American, and a Euro-American congregation, all of whose stated beliefs sound very similar. Does that mean that these local churches are completely alike? Certainly not. Their stated beliefs function as part of their sayings, but there is much more to their churches at the bottoms of their respective swamps.

The task of theologizing, then, becomes one of seeking to live into the beliefs, the claims themselves. This task sounds familiar to earnest religious people, but in this case the work can be described in some detail. It calls for critiquing submerged material on the basis of the theological saying—a task more easily (if you can pardon the pun) said than done. Most churches do not realize that their theological claims, as precious as they are, actually are important to them because of the particular relationship that they have with certain of the submerged materials. Theology and religion always are clothed in culture. So in order for a community of faith to discover if the religious beliefs (swamp sayings) will be central to their life, that community must test them. It must intentionally put those sayings to work in concrete situations. If the congregation perceives (and this point about perception is key) that the theological assertions work for them, then some of their submerged elements reflect those assertions in a useful way. In the development of church culture, the opposite also is true. If the congregation perceives that the beliefs do not work, it faces a crisis. Some members will leave, while those who remain must adapt their theological sayings. Either way, the mud in the swamp is affected.

In short, my junior high band teacher was almost right when she said, "Don't talk about it, do it!" Taking the Gospel seriously means holding up all of our church stuff before the Gospel's claims and seeking to discern where the stuff is linked to the mud. What are those unspoken assumptions tied to specific religious objects and behaviors? Have we made them idols, taking God's place? This is a spiritual community discipline that is especially challenging in American society, which promotes its dream in ideal economic and political terms.

Power, Gospel, and Culture

A third general observation from this chapter's discussion moves the matter of power one step further. If religious communities seek to utilize power in a countercultural way, what will it look like? If we accept that, at least in some way, the ways of God are not of this world, how do we imagine power operating? If we argue that power is evil by nature, we run the risk of self-deception, supposing that religious groups neither create nor wield power. A look at history should dispel such a naïve perception. Culture, as a studied discipline, helps us move between naiveté and cynicism.

To illustrate, I commend Eric Law's concise but profound discussion of what he calls "the Cycle of Gospel Living." This model blends cultural insight with theological clarity to point the way toward one kind of power sharing. Law's vision that "the church is to become the holy mountain on which people from diverse cultures shall not hurt or destroy each other" is not confined to culture in a narrow sense, but for any divisions between groups of people. Justice and power go together so that the power differentials—which sometimes are not conscious to those in power—can be balanced. When this happens, Law says, "People from different cultures [read also "various confluences of culture"] encounter each other with equal strength."[27]

The way that Law approaches this goal is by positing a cycle around which persons from different positions of power need to enter. For whites who are educated and comfortably placed in society, the entry point is symbolized by the cross, i.e., by giving up the power that they have. For people of color, the entry point is symbolized by the empty tomb, by resurrection, i.e., by receiving power. In church situations where diverse groups are represented, Law argues, it is theologically necessary for power to be shared in this way. What the giving and receiving actually looks like can depend upon the circumstances. For Law, one simple but effective way is for those perceived as powerful to invite those perceived as powerless to speak. "Mutual invitation" is a technique that congregations can learn to use, since there virtually always are perceptions of power difference in any church context or activity.[28]

Law's concept of the Cycle of Gospel Living does not mean that persons from conventionally powerful communities give up their power forever. That simply keeps the power concentrated with one group over that of another group. The reason that it is a cycle is that power, to be genuinely good for all, must be shared. One of the challenges for churches is to become a place where power is both received and given at all levels. This challenge will call for considerable intentional effort and attention to the use of skills designed for the purpose.[29] In the language of this chapter, the challenge is to assert a certain saying ("our church will share power"), start practicing certain behaviors—stuff—that will support the saying (mutual invitation at board meetings, worship-planning team that is not dominated by one person, etc.), and perceive that this new saying and new stuff does what the church wants it to do. At that point, some new submerged pieces in the church's cultural mud will be formed, pieces that strengthen—rather than weaken—the church's ministry vitality. In the metaphor of this book, alligators must learn to let other species in the swamp have a say. Otherwise, the swamp will lose the diversity that it needs to remain a thriving place to live. In the language of the church, the Cycle of Gospel Living shows us how to live out the Gospel call more fully, to realize "the vision of the Peaceable Realm."[30]

Advice for Alligators (This Means All of You!)

Space does not permit an extensive exploration of all the ways in which a cultural perspective on church and power can be understood and enabled. Let us turn again to the book's metaphor to suggest a few more insights. While the primary reader of this book might be a pastor, anyone concerned with the topic of religious community and power will find ways to use these suggestions.

Becoming an alligator. Pastors, especially, enter a new appointment or new call as the brand new creature in the swamp. Are they an alligator when they arrive? That depends. However, even if a new pastor perceives stuff that indicates power to the pastoral office, beware! Authority (which comes with office) often does not equate to power, especially at first. Pastors might have enjoyed flexing their alligator muscles in one part of the swamp, only to find out that they don't necessarily have that muscle in a different location. Perhaps the pastor who arrives is viewed by the members more as a raccoon or a crane—smaller, more agile, and more vulnerable to the swamp's residents. Or perhaps the pastor has become recognized as a powerful alligator in her congregation and assumes that she can wield the same bite in the church's neighborhood.

Many pastors report that they discover early in pastorates that things did not go as smoothly as they had imagined. It is very easy for alligators to get tangled up in the swamp if they don't know their way around. In another book, I have referred to this tangle as the pastor "stepping on a land mine." There I make the case for the pastor's need to develop "cultural capital," i.e., a respect and honoring of the church's culture that leads to congregational adoption.[31] In order to be seen by the congregation, or by the congregation's wider community, as one with power (and not just authority), pastors need to become alligators in every new situation. This task requires attention to learning more than the top two levels of that congregation's swamp—that is, the stuff and the sayings. It calls for a learning spirit to discern what is deeply submerged and how those unconscious elements inform the stuff. Anecdotally, pastors sometimes hear of this process as one of "earning your wings," "paying the rent," or "proving yourself." Its outcome is the congregation's respect, trust, and willingness to heed the pastor's words and actions. Then the pastor has a right to be called an alligator—and to act like one.

Alligators on the shore. One of the secondary claims put forth both in this chapter and the previous one is that alligators should not push their strength around. There are plenty of sayings (both theological and cultural) in the New Testament promoting an unassuming style of leading:

- "among the Gentiles those whom they recognize as their rules lord it over them,... But it is not so among you; but whoever wishes to be great among you must be your servant" (Mark 10:42b–43)
- "Do nothing from selfish ambition or conceit, but in humility regard others as better than yourselves" (Philippians 2:3)
- "Has not God chosen the poor in the world to be rich in faith...?" (James 2:5b)

As chapter two suggested, pastors who are not in touch with their alligator nature have a difficult time learning how to share power. We saw in the discussion of Eric Law's treatment of church and culture that specific techniques can be employed to demonstrate how serious we are about not lording it over others. As we listen to the Gospel, we are challenged to make a place for every alligator as well as all the other creatures who don't appear to have alligator power.

The alligator's bite. Major public discussion in the wider church these days has centered on the matter of pastoral integrity. Shocking cases of child abuse and other forms of clergy misconduct only serve to emphasize that church and society still hold strong submerged beliefs about the pastoral office being trustworthy. Does a pastor use the potential power from the pastoral office for good? This is a most serious matter that cannot be easily dismissed. The story of David and Bathsheba provides a tragic commentary to someone chosen by God who oversteps boundaries, flush with the success of power. In the framework of this chapter, the tragedy is not simply personal; the entire congregation and community are affected as well. Alligators need to learn to put the strength of their bite and the swing of their tail to good use.

Living together in the swamp. Political, economic, and social changes during the late modern period of American society have led to complex relationships between churches and their communities. Increasingly, society expects religious groups to contribute something of specific, concrete value to the neighborhoods and towns where they worship. Controversy over President George W. Bush's support of federal funds for faith-based social services illustrates recognition of this expectation. Clearly, the Gospel itself points followers in the direction of engaging their world in some manner. Churches that do nothing but keep to themselves seem out of step today.

Even if a church was not interested in some form of community engagement, the fact remains that it will be influenced by that very community. Thus, even at the lowest level, churches have to take their context into account. In what ways will they do so? How can a cultural perspective on congregation and community inform such an accounting?

The simplest answer to this question is that, whether it is recognized or not, churches are forced like every other organization to negotiate power with their wider community. One way that some churches negotiate is by offering their version of the faith to those who find themselves on the edges of society in general. Churches like these usually view themselves as only minimally affected by the confluence of their church's culture with that of their neighborhood or country. They might view themselves as lesser creatures in the swamp, seeking a safe place to live and hide from the alligators (who are perceived as always dangerous). Another way that some churches negotiate power is by minimizing the logjam potential between church and community. If the two respective cultural swamps are difficult to distinguish, that congregation basically represents its community. Alligators then are seen as magnanimous and good-hearted, publicly making room for all the other creatures but privately not always as trustworthy as would be hoped. Alligator fights often remain behind closed doors where none appear to be harmed, even when one wins and the other loses.

Somewhere between these two scenarios, congregations will discover themselves. In other words, the very nature of culture causes all churches to define some kind of relationship with the outside world. Those who do so with their eyes open (kind of like the way an alligator can skim the surface of the water) are better prepared to be honest about themselves and their opportunities for ministry.

Culture: Map and Compass in the Swamp

This chapter expounds the second of four views that are presented in this book on the church and power. Its aim is to help the reader wrestle not only with the multifaceted character of culture within and beyond the parish but also with how power does and should work. The conceptual framework outlined here is distilled from years of study, pastoral reflection, teaching, training, and writing. Like any major shift of models, this culture theory takes time to learn and use. However, I would argue that we have no choice these days but to learn new things. The world into which I was born is fading and a new one is emerging. I don't use a typewriter anymore, and I also seek to keep learning in other ways. Alfred North Whitehead once wrote, "The pure conservative is fighting against the essence of the universe."[32] So don't be surprised if you feel that you still have a lot to learn about power!

Churches (and any religious community) can be compared to swamps; pastors can be compared to alligators. How pastors and churches understand and exercise their power depends in large part upon the deep, submerged beliefs located in the mud of their cultural swamps. This chapter gives you tools to see power in a fresh way and apply what you have learned to the pastoral role and the congregation's life. The following two chapters build upon one of the themes of this chapter, namely, that the world beyond the congregation has a life of its own and yet can be beneficially engaged. Alligators live everywhere!

A Craft for Navigating the Swamp: Alligators in the Regime

by Harvey K. Newman

4

Not All Alligators Meet in the Boardroom

Three male alligators are getting together to tee off at the local country club. Al asks, "Where do you think we ought to build the new convention center? I think it should be near that parking deck I own." One of the others responds, "Yes, that sounds like a great place to enlarge our convention facility. We could attract more and larger groups. Maybe bring some new jobs to the area, and certainly help with the sales tax revenue. I'll discuss it with the mayor next week."

What is going on in the scene above? The alligators were supposed to have a *formal* meeting at city hall or in the boardroom of an important corporation to make decisions. Instead, they are having an *informal* gathering on the golf course to decide how things will get done. Sometimes, when the formal meeting does take place, it is just to ratify the agreement made when a small group of the most influential alligators have talked among themselves in their private, less formal gatherings.

Like some humans, alligators often meet in informal settings to make important decisions. These settings might include a private club, a gym, a bar, or wherever creatures gather and talk. How do these alligators have the power to make decisions during informal gatherings on a golf course? Is politics always about the backroom deals that shape decisions? This chapter describes how important decisions often get made in swamps, towns, and cities everywhere. The process of making local decisions through informal processes has been described as an "urban regime." In this chapter, the idea of a regime is used to provide a sturdy craft for understanding and navigating the roots, stumps, and mud of the swamps where these decisions are made.

The idea of a regime is a helpful way for people in churches to know how decisions are made within their local community. This is useful if Christians are going to become more active and effective participants in politics. The former Speaker of the House, Tip O'Neill, frequently remarked that all politics is local, so understanding the regime that operates in a community is crucial for people in churches who wish to act as responsible Christians in the public square.

Regime Politics

A half century ago, the study of politics involved the analysis of formal structures of decision making. Students examined organization charts from city hall to see where the lines of authority connected one square on the chart to another. More recently, this study has taken a different turn to recognize how many decisions are made based on the tacit, informal agreements of people who interact with one another on a regular basis. The study of these kinds of informal coalitions is called regime politics. Political scientist Clarence Stone defined an urban regime as "the informal arrangements by which public bodies and private interests function together in order to be able to make and carry out governing decisions."[1] This notion of regime politics is helpful in finding one's way through the swamp that often describes a local community.

The first step in using regime theory to understand a town or city is to determine who the major participants are in local decision making. In the example of the alligators on the golf course, these may be important business leaders. The cast of characters may vary from place to place and may change over time within the same place. In 1950, when Floyd Hunter studied decision making in Atlanta, he identified the forty most influential people in the city. Of these, twenty-nine were business leaders, so that leaders from government, community groups, and others represented only eleven of the forty. These forty leaders included only five females and one African American.[2] In recent years, the same kind of list would be very different. One constant would probably be that a majority of the leading decision makers would be from the private sector. On the one hand, most local governments do not have the ability to accomplish their goals without the participation and cooperation of businesses. Since city governments by themselves lack the resources to govern and carry out important policies, local officials feel that they must keep existing businesses and try to attract new investment within their community in order to maintain local services and fiscal well-being.

On the other hand, businesses get involved in local politics for a variety of reasons. First, it may add to their profits to be part of a growing community—more investment usually translates into more jobs and people that can contribute to the prosperity of the city. Another reason for business involvement in local politics is to increase the value of their property. Local affairs are also considered valuable for the positive image of a business within a community, which can also increase profits. There are often close personal ties between local elected public officials and business leaders. After all, many mayors and council members serve as part-time public officials while retaining jobs in business organizations. Even full-time public officials often emerge from business backgrounds before their entry into the public sector, and many of these same individuals return to business after leaving office. These types of relationships ensure that local governments most often pursue policies directed toward growth and investment in the local community. Political scientist Paul Peterson describes these favored local government programs as developmental policies.[3]

Local governments, most often with the support of business allies, pursue an agenda of these developmental policies in order to attract or retain investment in the local area. It is generally assumed that the role of the public sector is to provide the setting for businesses to operate successfully within the boundaries of the government. For a city or town this means providing a good climate for business as well as incentives for business retention or attraction. After all, the local tax digest depends upon business investments in the community in order to provide revenues for public services as well as employment for local residents. Local public officials who are openly hostile or even indifferent to the needs of the private sector face the prospect of businesses relocating to other cities that might be more welcoming. This competition between towns and cities of all sizes for investment is another reason local governments must pursue development policies.

Tourism as an Economic Development Policy

The alligators on the golf course were discussing one type of economic development policy. Both favored building the larger convention center in order to attract more meetings to the city. Urban places both large and small are using variations of this policy to bring tourists with their dollars to cities and towns. Places that are fortunate enough to have natural attractions are attempting to take advantage of features such as the ocean, a riverfront, or a lake shore to draw more leisure- or recreation-oriented visitors. Other locations are seeking to become conference or convention locations and to attract more business travelers. A lack of natural attractions is not an obstacle for cities wishing to convert whatever assets they have into tourist amenities.[4] These places must build the collection of facilities required for conferences or conventions.

The types of facilities that cities build to attract tourists are remarkably similar from place to place throughout the United States. One obvious need is for a hall large enough to host conventions or conferences. These facilities are almost always financed and built by the public sector as part of the infrastructure needed to attract visitors. Other common features of the tourist spaces in most cities include sports arenas for major or minor league games that can provide entertainment for locals as well as visitors. Festival malls such as Faneuil Hall in Boston, Harbor Place in Baltimore, and Underground Atlanta are also important components for a city's tourism business. These festival malls are developed to provide space to attract recreational shoppers rather than a resident population seeking mundane necessities. Most of these are the result of public subsidies by local governments in partnership with private investors. One of the earliest of these festival malls, Faneuil Hall in Boston required less than 21 percent public-sector support, while Underground Atlanta received more than 80 percent of its funding from the public sector.[5] Civic leaders hope that large public-sector investments in meeting halls, sports arenas, and festival malls will encourage the spending of private dollars to build hotels, restaurants, and amusements for tourists. Another hope is that these public and private investments will act as magnets to draw free-spending tourists to the community.

In most towns and cities the efforts to attract visitors has replaced the earlier economic development policy of "smokestack chasing" by attempting to lure manufacturing plants to relocate from another town or region. For example, beginning soon after the Civil War, southern cities sought to entice the owners of textile mills to relocate their mills from the northeast. Many of these mills moved to the south, taking advantage of cheaper labor and land costs as well as the subsidies offered by cities and states. More recently, many of these same plants have closed and relocated to other countries, leaving once-thriving southern communities scrambling to attract new forms of investment through economic development policies focused on tourism.

So, we've agreed on our proposal to the mayor, yes?

Where the competition used to exist among towns to attract a textile mill or other type of industrial plant, many community leaders now seek tourists to visit, sleep, eat, drink, buy souvenirs, and perhaps find the locality pleasant enough to want to stay and do business. Local strategies vary from place to place, but communities as diverse as Flint, Michigan and Marion, South Carolina have sought to replace lost industrial jobs with tourist attractions. Local leaders are willing to spend public funds to provide the facilities for tourists in the hope that private-sector investments and jobs will follow.

The examples of Flint and Marion provide a cautionary lesson for many other localities as they seek to become tourist destinations. Flint's tourist theme park called AutoWorld and Marion's amphitheater both failed to attract visitors in large numbers. The experience of these two communities suggests that some places are not attractive destinations for visitors. These towns and cities lacked natural attractions, and also failed to provide the image of a place that visitors wished to experience. For some municipalities, it is a difficult task to construct the amenities needed for a tourist destination and expect visitors to come. Even with a theme park or a conference center plus nearby hotels, restaurants, and other amenities needed to attract visitors, some places are not regarded as favorable destinations by tourists. Yet, to leaders of towns and cities everywhere, the possibilities of free-spending tourists coming to their communities provides a powerful stimulus to economic development policies of one kind or another designed to attract visitors. The result has been described as a "field of dreams" approach to economic development policy, with local business and political leaders believing, "if we build it, the tourists will come."[6]

Regime Decisions

Returning to our threesome of alligators on the golf course, how are these local business leaders able to get things done? How are these particular alligators able to translate their conversation about the building of a new convention center into a decision that is both made and implemented? When Hunter studied decision making in Atlanta in 1950, he described a pattern in which a small group of business and professional people were able to dominate decisions in the city. Hunter called this pattern of decision making "elitism," and for Hunter and his many followers, the pattern of communities controlled by a small elite group became the prevailing explanation of how cities are governed.[7] This small group of leaders would meet informally to decide on policies such as the use of transportation plans to increase the space of downtown. For example, one such private group of business leaders in Atlanta began planning the city's expressway system in 1948 (before the federal interstate highway system) with a curve in the north-south freeway that would serve two purposes: The land inside the bend would expand the space available for the expansion of downtown businesses, and the highway itself would form a barrier between downtown and the east Atlanta African American residential area.[8] Once the influential group of business leaders reached an informal agreement, they involved the mayor and other appropriate public officials to ratify and implement the agreement.

Other scholars disagreed with Hunter's claim that a small elite group of local business leaders was responsible for running a city. In his study of New Haven, Robert Dahl observed a variety of different individuals and groups participating in local decisions. One set of people would likely be involved in decisions involving transportation, while another set might make decisions in education, so that relatively different groups were involved in each policy area. Dahl called this pattern of governing "pluralism" after the diverse groups involved in each policy area.[9] The result was a vigorous debate between the elitists who followed Hunter and the pluralists who agreed with Dahl and saw more diversity among the participants in local decision making.

The debate ended in 1989 with the publication of *Regime Politics* by Clarence Stone. On one level, the study of decisions such as the construction of the new convention center by our golfing alligators might appear to be an elitist perspective. The two are certainly among the largest and most powerful in the swamp. However, Stone is careful to distinguish between his position and that of Hunter's elitist point of view. For one thing, while these alligators are often in a position to influence the outcome of decisions, they do not always get their way. Stone agrees to an extent with Dahl's pluralist point of view that decision making in a city is a process made complicated by a larger number of participants than the elitists might suggest. Thus, many smaller alligators of both genders could band together and influence decisions against the wishes of the larger male alligators.

Against the argument that Stone is taking the side of the pluralists, there is the importance of business groups within the regime. While Stone acknowledges that business groups do not always get their way, he understands that they are generally better organized and have more resources than other regime participants. Other groups who might take part in regime decisions could include labor unions, nonprofit organizations, and religious groups such as churches, synagogues, and mosques. Few of these can match the resources of private-sector businesses that have the people as well as the equipment and capital to influence local decisions. Two questions for thought and discussion are: Who are the organized groups that participate in decision making in your local community? Do all of these groups participate equally, or is leadership on most issues provided by business organizations?

Stone has a different view from either the elitists or the pluralists on what business leaders *do* with their resources as decisions are made. Groups that participate in a regime do not use their resources to control decision making. Instead, the resources are used to produce cooperation among regime participants. This is an important distinction because both the pluralists and elitists examined the domination of local decision making and the costs of controlling the process. Regime politics is a study of how groups work together to achieve, in Stone's words, "cooperation of the kind that can bring together people based in different sectors of a community's institutional life and that enables a coalition of actors to make and support a set of governing decisions.... it is an examination of how that cooperation is maintained when confronted with an ongoing process of social change, a continuing influx of new actors, and potential break-downs through conflict or indifference."[10]

The Growth Machine

Stone refers to this process of groups working together to make and implement decisions as civic cooperation. How do leaders such as the three golfing alligators achieve the cooperation among groups needed to get things done within the swamp? Stone's term "civic cooperation" describes the process of coordinating efforts across the boundaries of groups within a regime.[11] Businesses, organizations, and individuals that support regime decisions are likely to benefit from their cooperation with the process. Those who are shut out or oppose the decisions being made usually suffer consequences for their actions. Incentives for participation might include access to employment, contracts, foundation support, and other benefits. Usually this system of incentives is based on an agreement among all the regime participants on the benefits of growth to the city. Sociologists John Logan and Harvey Molotch described this coalition as an urban growth machine in which all of the parties stand to benefit from local growth policies. Important growth-machine participants would include business people who are involved in property investing, development, and real estate finance. This group includes lawyers, bankers, and others who benefit from increasing the value of land and buildings within a city. Less obvious growth-machine participants would be local media such as newspapers, radio, and television stations that profit from growth through increased subscribers, listeners, and viewers as well as increased advertising revenue. Local public officials generally support the goals of bringing growth to the community as it tends to reflect favorably on their record in office and provides the benefits of increased tax revenues and employment. Utility companies that provide electricity, gas, water, and cable services stand to benefit from a growing community that brings new customers and increased demand for their services.[12]

In addition to the major players in the urban growth machine, Logan and Molotch identify a list of other supporters of local growth policies. These are labor unions, professional sports teams, and cultural institutions such as universities, museums, theaters, and symphonies in a locality. A growing community provides additional patrons for a symphony or a museum as well as additional financial supporters. Sports teams can increase their fan base within a growing city. Universities can also promote growth as they are increasingly regarded as engines of economic development for towns and cities. Prominent examples include the role of Stanford University in the development of the Silicon Valley in California and the three universities (Duke, the University of North Carolina at Chapel Hill, and North Carolina State in Raleigh) that form the three points of the Research Triangle. Other growth-machine participants may include corporate business leaders, self-employed professionals, and small retailers.[13]

An interesting question is the role that churches and other religious organizations play within local growth machines. Many small congregations form an important part of the neighborhoods in which they are located. Members who live in the area often participate in the activities of the congregation and develop close attachments to other members and to the institution itself, as it is the place where births, weddings, funerals, and other events are observed over the course of years. Larger congregations may, however, sometimes find themselves at odds with the residents of the area in which their church is located. As congregations seek additional land for parking or buildings, neighbors may oppose these expansion plans as the church will bring unwanted traffic and congestion to the area. At other times, churches may act like full-fledged participants in the local growth machine in the pursuit of profits from the value of their land.

Logan and Molotch mention churches as potential participants in a city's growth machine with the comment that, "Downtown churches are looking to the heavens for financial returns, arranging to sell air rights over their imposing edifices to developers of nearby parcels."[14] They were describing the controversy over the proposed sale of the air rights above a building owned by St. Bartholomew Episcopal Church in Manhattan. The sale would have earned millions of dollars for the endowment of the church's social ministries in New York City. Instead, it generated conflict between the pastor of the church and developers, who supported the proposal, and many members of the congregation and advocates of historic preservation, who opposed the sale that would have allowed construction of a skyscraper above the carriage house behind the historic church. In the end, the congregation decided against selling the air rights to the developer.

Another example of a church participating in the local growth machine took place in 1988, when the First Baptist Church of Atlanta accepted an offer of $62 million for its sixteen acres of land and buildings in the Midtown area of the city to move to a northern suburb known as Dunwoody. The issue was raised by the pastor one Sunday and voted on the next week. No one was allowed to raise questions about the decision to sell the church and move. The pastor commented that God is for growth and anyone opposed is "under Satan's influence."[15] This case raises an important issue of the extent to which other congregations participate as active members of a local growth machine. One discussion would be whether local congregations in your community profited from the sale of land and buildings. If so, how have these profits been used? St. Bartholomew proposed to use their profits to endow their church's social ministry, while First Baptist purchased new land and moved to the suburbs. Another topic for discussion is how expansion plans of a local congregation affect its surrounding neighborhood. Are the new buildings or parking lots going to increase traffic and congestion in the area? Also, how are the neighbors reacting to the congregation's development plans? The answers to these questions may suggest some of the ways churches participate in the local growth machine.

Reward, Punishment, or Cooperation?

Usually, the businesses who are members of a local growth machine are organized to promote local development through groups such as Chambers of Commerce, Convention and Visitors Bureaus, and other civic associations. Public officials who favor growth coalition interests receive campaign support and media endorsements. Nonprofit organization directors also depend on the financial support of individual business leaders as well as foundations that are responsible to many of these same business interests. This creates the system of selective incentives to promote civic cooperation that Stone describes with the phrase, "go along to get along."[16]

Those who realize the benefits of going along with the coalition know that cooperation is rewarded and noncooperation is punished. Punishment may take the form of withholding financial support or simply ignoring those who do not go along with the wishes of major regime participants. Either consequence can be harmful to groups such as small nonprofit organizations that can be shut out of access to important sources of support and publicity for their programs. Individuals also take part in the same system of incentives to go along to get along. Another question for discussion is how might individual members or a congregation as a whole be either rewarded for supporting a regime decision or punished for failing to do so?

The system of rewards and punishment that are part of civic cooperation do not just apply to individuals seeking personal opportunities within the growth coalition. It also extends to the broader question of how to further more complex projects and to promote policy initiatives. Advancing a project or program usually requires many forms of support, ranging from money needed from several sources, endorsements, favorable publicity, and help from knowledgeable experts on how to avoid technical and legal pitfalls. Business leaders are typically the source for this kind of assistance. The availability of their aid is usually indispensable for a local project or proposal to move forward. Likewise, opposition from these sources can kill a project.[17] This system of civic cooperation gives business leaders an advantage when it comes to influencing local decisions. It does not mean that Hunter was correct in describing municipal decision making by a small elite.

Opposition to policies and programs favored by business interests frequently surfaces in towns and cities. Opponents face the difficulty of organizing themselves and producing enough resources to counter the efforts of a local regime. Remember that resources can take the form of people as well as money and other material. Thus, a large number of smaller alligators can be effective in opposing the wishes of a smaller number of larger ones. For example, opposition can be expressed through votes in a local election. This can thrust forward a candidate who opposes the existing policies of a regime or its leadership. Once the election is over, the challenge becomes one of effective governance. This will require building coalitions to make decisions rather than the relatively simple task of mounting opposition during an election.

One example of an election coalition may be seen in the 1973 campaign of Maynard Jackson for mayor of Atlanta. In his race against incumbent Sam Massell, Jackson put together a coalition of two sizable groups in the city. The first was the new majority of black citizens who responded to his progressive agenda of affirmative action and minority contracting. The second was a coalition of mostly young white voters who were part of an emerging neighborhood movement that opposed plans by the Georgia Department of Transportation and business leaders to build an expressway project known as I-485. The proposed roadway would run through several older neighborhoods as it connected downtown with Stone Mountain in the eastern suburb of DeKalb County. Jackson put together a successful electoral coalition of black voters and white neighborhood activitists in order to defeat Mayor Massell. Once in office, however, the problem of implementing his policy agenda in the face of business opposition proved difficult. Jackson's years as mayor were spent trying to repair relationships with business leaders. This was needed to provide the civic cooperation that would enable the traditional partnership between city hall and business leaders to continue to function in the city. Civic cooperation is a kind of glue that binds together participants in a regime.

The lesson of civic cooperation to build a governing coalition within the regime was not lost on Jackson's successor, Andrew Young. Young was familiar to voters after serving as congressional representative of the city and as ambassador to the United Nations under President Jimmy Carter. He ran for mayor with the support of Maynard Jackson and a solid majority among African American residents. Most of the white downtown business leaders favored his opponent. The day after his election in 1981, Young addressed a luncheon of business leaders and told them, "I didn't get elected with your help, but I can't govern without you."[18] With this speech and his subsequent actions, Young won the support of the city's business leadership. Throughout his eight years as mayor, Andrew Young remained a strong partner with the city's business community in the traditional regime coalition. This occasionally put him in conflict with the interests of low-income African American residents of the city as well as white neighborhood activists. Young was able to pursue his agenda of economic development for the city with the active cooperation of business leaders. This resulted in the accomplishment of complex tasks such as the redevelopment of the downtown tourist attraction known as Underground Atlanta. If Logan and Molotch are correct, most mayors follow the pattern of Andrew Young of Atlanta in working closely with business leaders as part of the local growth coalition.

It seems obvious that the golfing alligators are part of the local growth machine in their swamp. If so, what other lessons can be learned from our pair of alligators about regime decision making? One important lesson is *how* the participants in the regime get things done. Our golfing alligators are large male business leaders. To a degree these leaders control the agenda for the local community— whether the community is a swamp or a city. Once the discussion starts on *where* to locate the new convention center, the debate already assumes that it is a good idea to build the facility. This ignores the larger issue of whether or not a new facility should be built. In this instance, control over the agenda helps to shape the outcome, so that little discussion is held on if a new convention facility should be built. Should, for example, the new facility be built on land owned by Al, our golfing alligator, or on the site of the older facility after it was demolished to make way for the new? No one seems to question whether convention visitors will want to come to town once the facility is built. It is often difficult for local leaders to recognize that the swamp they call home is not a place tourists want to visit no matter what kinds of attractions are constructed.

The private, informal discussion between our two alligators is, in itself, an important step in local decision making. It is increasingly recognized that the use of language by those in positions of power has the ability to shape actions. Robert Beauregard suggested that the words of business and political leaders in a city have ethical consequences.[19] Those who are in a position to shape the discourse can use their position to define the actions of others within a locality.[20] This provides another powerful resource for those who are in a position to use it. Even though the discussions are held in informal settings, these conversations may later be favorably reported by local media who are generally supportive of growth policies and participants in regime decisions.

Newspapers, for example, can play a neutral role in the discussion of which site to build the new convention center, but local media almost always favor policies that promote growth. In this way, the news media can also frame the discussion to avoid, or at least minimize, the issue of whether the city needs a new convention facility. Reporters can be sent out to investigate the pros and cons of each potential location—to build on the site of the parking lot owned by Al or to tear down the smaller old convention center and build the new facility on that site. Other issues such as job training for the underemployed or those without jobs and improving the quantity and quality of low- and moderate-income housing are more difficult to place on the agenda for public discussion within the community.

Changing the Regime

Does this mean that the smaller creatures of the swamp should become resigned to the fact that the large, male alligators are usually going to get their way just because of their size? Stone says that regime participants can change their minds about issues if they are made aware of opposing points of view. This is a process of changing the regime that Stone calls "social learning."[21] Perhaps one way to describe social learning is with the story of the mule and the 2' × 4' board. There was a time not so long ago when mules provided much of the power for agriculture in the U.S. These creatures were known for their stubbornness. This meant that sometimes, when a mule refused to budge, the farmer had to hit the mule in the head with a 2'× 4' in order to get his attention. Changing the regime can be a bit like that. It is sometimes necessary to hit the mules in the head with a board in order to get their attention if you want them to go in a different direction. This is the process of social learning that may be required to get the attention of some rather stubborn mules. Social learning is the process of opening the eyes of regime participants to points of view that might not have occurred to them otherwise.

Social learning can be done in a variety of ways without resorting to the use of 2' × 4's. One strategy is to provide regime leaders with information and education that they might not get from other sources. A simple strategy is to bring attention to an issue that needs the attention of local leaders. Individuals and groups can write letters, lobby elected officials, or even hold demonstrations to call attention to important issues. Another approach is through active participation on committees, boards, and commissions set up by local government.

One example of social learning took place during Andrew Young's two terms as mayor of Atlanta. From the moment of his election, Young formed a strong partnership with business leaders to promote development in the city. Some Atlanta residents who were left on the sidelines of regime decisions during the early years of Young's tenure as mayor were advocates of historic preservation. Older commercial buildings and homes were usually torn down if they stood in the way of new development.

During his first four years in office, Mayor Young opposed historic preservation, saying that it would limit development in the city. He vetoed proposed legislation designed to save older buildings in Atlanta, arguing that preservation regulations might slow investment in the city by scaring off developers. Without the ordinance in place, the apartments and several other historic structures were torn down during 1986.[22]

Protests over the demolition of these older buildings continued to mount, and, in response, Mayor Young agreed to form a task force to develop a new preservation policy for the city. Young served as a member of the task force along with a mix of developers, preservation advocates, and members of the city council. National experts on historic preservation and others appeared before the task force as the group met over the next two years. At the end of the process, the task force members developed a consensus in support of a new and stronger historic preservation ordinance for Atlanta. Both the preservationists and the developers compromised on some issues in order to arrive at the final policy proposal. What is more significant, during the process, the two sides developed lines of communication and a level of trust that would be needed to secure passage of the proposed ordinance by the city council. Finally, in June 1989, the city council passed the new historic preservation ordinance, and Mayor Young signed the legislation.

In Stone's terms, social learning took place over the course of the meetings by the task force members, so that both sides came to understand one another. Before the meetings of the task force, the participants on the two sides had viewed one another with suspicion, if not hostility. As a result of the process, the developers and Mayor Young were able to see the point of view of the preservationists—that saving older buildings made economic sense and also contributed toward making the city a more interesting place. Stone described social learning as the capacity for members of the regime to inform themselves and to understand more diverse points of view. In this way, decisions were not made exclusively within the confines of the selective incentives provided to regime participants.

The example of the task force on historic preservation shows how social learning can work. In this case, social learning provided openness to more issues raised by the community with the potential to change the regime into a more inclusive coalition. After years of being able to ignore the wishes of preservationists, the process experienced by the task force resulted in the passage of the new ordinance and its approval by Mayor Young. As a result, older buildings continue to enjoy a higher level of protection as well as an improved procedure for dealing with threats to historic structures. Demolition of a building with historic significance is no longer done without a careful review of its merits and its potential for economic return for the owner. This was part of the compromise that resulted from the extensive meetings of the task force and the social learning by developers and elected public officials. Another question for discussion is what can church members do to provide social learning to their local regime? Is it better to share information in formal or informal ways?

Social learning can produce the benefits of an expanded range of vision by important decision makers. This can result in broader participation in the regime and, often, a change in regime policies. For a group of smaller reptiles to change the regime of the large male alligators requires that the smaller animals must know who the key participants are in the local regime. Armed with the names of important local business and political leaders, the smaller alligators can proceed to the next step—organization. The old saying about their being strength in numbers applies to efforts to change local policies. First, there have to be large numbers of creatures wanting change, and, in addition, these animals must be well organized. This may mean strengthening existing organizations or perhaps forming new ones.

Change Through Alliances

Organizational strength also comes from the willingness to form alliances with other partners in the swamp. Here the first rule is "you help me and I'll help you," as creatures representing varied interest groups join together in coalitions to secure benefits from local political action. Coalition politics can come from alliances between unlikely partners. Even though these coalitions often make for strange animals sharing the same beds, it is crucial to increase support by forming these types of informal alliances. This means that the second rule of political coalitions is "politics makes strange bedfellows."[23] These informal coalitions can be effective in seeking to influence decisions within a local regime.

Chester Hartman provided a classic study of coalition politics in San Francisco over the building of the proposed Yerba Buena convention center.[24] The plan for the new convention center was advanced by a powerful coalition of business leaders. The development advocates included tourist-oriented businesses, the local Hotel Owners Association, the Chamber of Commerce, and others who thought that the new convention center would be good for business in San Francisco. This coalition was well represented in the official local government agency known as the San Francisco Redevelopment Agency (SFRA), which was responsible for urban renewal and redevelopment in the city. The new center would be located in an area near downtown that consisted of low-income housing, warehouses, and older industrial plants that was known as Yerba Buena. The pro-development coalition funded studies designed to demonstrate how much San Francisco would benefit from the proposed center; they lobbied city officials to give the necessary approvals and actively participated in planning the project. The prospect of jobs created by the construction of the new center attracted the support of labor unions, contractors, and others who joined the coalition supporting the convention facility. This familiar growth machine coalition came together around what each of the participants considered their own self-interest in what they wanted, not only for themselves but for what they regarded as good for the city as well.

Once the SFRA started the process of acquiring land, moving residents, and demolishing buildings in the Yerba Buena area, a reaction against the pro-growth coalition began. Neighborhood residents, who were mostly poor and elderly, established an organization known as Tenants and Owners in Opposition to Redevelopment (TOOR) to represent their interests. TOOR members demonstrated against the proposed convention center. They also filed a lawsuit to block the project, claiming that the center would destroy the neighborhood that had long been their home. TOOR argued that if the development did take place, area residents should receive new affordable housing near the old neighborhood, as well as social services, open space, and a voice in planning how their future neighborhood would be built.

The members of TOOR seemed like an uneven match for the well-organized pro-growth coalition. The group reached out to form their own coalition with partners that included environmentalists opposed to the development of the convention center and a tax payer group who feared that the financing of the proposed convention center would increase local property taxes. Together these diverse opponents of the Yerba Buena Center were able to bring the project to a temporary halt. During this interval, the members of TOOR struck a compromise with the pro-growth coalition. TOOR ended its litigation against the city in return for its support of the proposed convention center. In return, TOOR received funding for affordable housing in the area as well as relocation benefits and improved social services. The convention center project was scaled down in size, allowing more open space in the area, which had been one of the concerns of the environmentalists. The smaller size of the project also reduced the cost of financing the center, which had been the focus of the taxpayer group.

What are the lessons of the Yerba Buena case study for the understanding of coalition politics? First, successful coalition building can influence local decisions. The rather strange coalition of opponents found enough strength in their numbers to change the outcome of the process in their favor. While the coalition did not succeed in stopping the project, it did have a positive influence on the outcome. Second, the results of the process showed the willingness of all the participants to compromise. Neither side got all that it had initially wanted, but the results reflected the interests of many more of the city's residents than represented by the pro-growth coalition or by the opposing groups alone. Next, the Yerba Buena case shows the influence of informal coalitions in local decision making. The city charter does not recognize the importance of business interests or organized citizen groups in shaping policy. Yet, the informal coalitions were central to the process of shaping how the convention center would be built. The interests of the well-financed business organizations were important, but their strength and size did not guarantee that they would get their way.

A well-organized, often diverse coalition opposed to a particular development project can influence the outcome in significant ways. In Stone's terms, this coalition can provide the social learning to change regime decisions. Finally, Hartman's case study is typical of the struggles that take place in towns and cities everywhere. While the names of the projects and the participants may differ, coalition politics produce the drama that takes place in every swamp. For discussion, is there an issue that you or your congregation wishes to influence? If so, with whom might you cooperate as allies? What informal coalitions can you form to increase your influence on local decision making?

Urban Citizenship

One important reason to read the newspaper every day is to learn about what issues are important within the community of your swamp. But, arming yourself with this information is merely an initial step. Local politics should not be a spectator sport that you watch from the sidelines. It calls for both individual and group participation. The more people who take an active part in local politics, the more representative and democratic your town or city's decision making is likely to be. Most citizens fail to realize just how important local politics is to their lives, and that we all have responsibilities as urban citizens. From earliest childhood most residents of the United States are trained for citizenship. In school children recite the pledge of allegiance to the United States, while they learn about the history and government of our nation and our state. At the same time, we give very little attention to developing citizens who are loyal to their local government. No class of young students stand and place their

Whoops! I guess we need to
include raccoon in this plan.

hands over their hearts in order to recite a pledge of allegiance to
Nashville, Portland, Milwaukee, or any other local government.

Another sad fact is that few residents even know what their local
government does for them. It could be argued that local politics does
more to determine the quality of a resident's life than any other level
of government. This is not to minimize the importance of the national government and its role in defending our shores and representing
the U.S. in relations with other countries. State governments also play

a significant role in exercising powers not specifically delegated to the federal government. One of those important state powers is creating local governments. But, local governments are responsible for those issues that most directly affect the quality of our day-to-day lives. The list of services provided by local governments includes public safety (police and fire protection), parks, recreation, streets, sidewalks, water treatment, sewers, trash collection, and education as well as the regulation of land use and the condition of housing. These are crucial things that touch our lives every day, which are generally ignored or given little attention as long as they are performed as a matter of routine. Only when the transit system breaks down, the sanitation workers go on strike, or we somehow experience an interruption in our services from local government that we notice how much each of us depends on these things that we normally take for granted.

Questions for discussion might include the following: First, what services does local government (city or county) provide in your community? Are these services provided in an effective manner? Is their distribution equitable? If you decide that there could be improvements in the services or the way in which they are delivered, what can you do to change the situation? Finally, what are your obligations as a citizen of your local community?

As much as the routine services of local government affect our lives, we also need to take into account how our lives are touched by the kind of development policies and other decisions made by town, city, or county governments. The ways in which these decisions are made in each community, regardless of size, constitute the local regime. The number of participants involved in making these policy decisions can vary from a minimum of two large alligators upward to include as many citizens as possible.

Theological Considerations

As people of faith, each of us has a special obligation to participate actively in community decision making. John Calvin taught that human beings are called to live within a set of social relationships. As Andre Bieler described Calvin's ideas, the Christian life is by its very nature a communal phenomenon. Government is an indispensable part of the social life in which believers participate. According to this doctrine, the duty of Christians is to abolish the divisions that separate people from one another—the rich from the poor, Greeks from Jews, or men from women. Bieler summarized Calvin's views by saying, "when Christians are aware of the responsibility flowing from their faith, they are under obligation to participate actively in political life."[25]

This requirement of political activity for the fulfillment of the Christian life is expressed in three ways. First, each individual Christian should be personally engaged in setting up a Christian community within the city and seeing to it that this religious community is, as far as possible, faithful to the gospel. Secondly, each Christian should be involved in political action with the objective of bettering social life through legal and institutional means. Finally, the Christian should refuse to follow the requirements of the government when it imposes duties that are incompatible with the demands of the gospel. Calvin has rightly been described as a conservative reformer because he insisted that it was the Christian's duty to continually reform both state and church.[26] The goal of the Christian's participation in government is to promote social justice. Commenting on Psalm 82:3 ("Give justice to the weak and the orphan, maintain the right of the lowly and the destitute...."), Calvin wrote, "a just and well-regulated government will be distinguished for maintaining the rights of the poor and afflicted."[27] These admonitions provide a powerful motivation for members of the reformed tradition to be actively involved in the affairs of local government.

Christians are also under special obligation to not only take a personal role in community governance but also to encourage others to participate in regime decisions. The New Testament makes it clear that all people, without distinction, should be brought to the table where community decisions are made. In other words, the regime ought to include as many people as possible. This is an important perspective—that church members themselves should not only participate in community affairs, but also they should encourage others. Members of the community of faith should not be part of the politics of *exclusion,* but, rather, the politics of *inclusion.* Those involved in the regime should not be limited to those who might be considered "righteous," but we should try to bring as many as possible to the table or wherever the discussions of important issues affecting the community are held.

Faith and Regime

Perhaps in this setting, the decision on the new convention center will not be made on the basis of *where* the facility ought to be located. Then, the discussion of the issue would not be limited to our pair of large male alligators chatting on the golf course. (This might, in itself, be an argument in favor of more inclusive memberships in private golf clubs.) With more people brought into the discussions the question will certainly be raised *if* the community needs a new convention center. Who would stand to benefit from the proposed new facility? Would the new facility affect low-income residents? Would it create new jobs, and, if so, how many and what kind of employment would the convention center generate? Would the facility bring in revenue from tourist dollars? What evidence is there to indicate that large numbers of tourists will want to come to our city? What would a new facility cost? How would it be financed? Would voters have a chance to approve both the construction and the financing of the convention center? In most towns and cities, decisions such as these are made behind closed doors among development authorities that are shielded from public review. Would taxpayers be responsible for paying any shortfall if rental income from the use of the facility turns out to be less than anticipated? These are the kind of questions that a fuller and more open discussion of the convention center proposal ought to have.

People of faith need to be personally involved in these kinds of discussions, and they have a responsibility to bring others to the table to participate as well. Broader regime participation could provide the kind of social learning that Stone suggested. This would bring changes in the regime itself and in the kinds of discussions that are carried on when decisions are made. Stone's book, *Regime Politics,* is dominated by an image of society that lacks consensus. People are not bound together by an integrating body of thought, a shared idea of the world, or even a set of norms and values that most have in common. Instead, society is loosely bound together at best, and usually fragmented into an arena such as a city (or swamp) where interest groups must be brought together in order to produce any sort of policy result. The process of making decisions is the task of bringing together enough resources to influence, first, policy making and, then, policy implementation. Governance takes place by the act of bringing groups together in order to act.[28]

The view of society in *Regime Politics* seems remarkably consistent with that of the New Testament. According to Paul's letters, the mission of believers is to reconcile others to faith in Christ. In the letter to the church in Ephesus, Paul reminds his readers that at one time they were *separated* from Christ, *alienated* from the commonwealth of Israel, and *strangers* to the covenants of promise, having no hope and without God in the world. "But now in Christ Jesus you who once were far off have been brought near...." But through Jesus, "you are no longer strangers and aliens, but you are citizens with the saints and also members of the household of God..." (Ephesians 2:12–9) This mission of bringing others to participate at the table where decisions are made can be seen as part of the ministry of reconciliation. The requirement is to bring together those who are separated, alienated, and strangers by building connections between people. We need this kind of reconciliation because the nature of our society is one in which people are alienated, cut off from one another. The strangers are brought in to become recognized as fellow citizens and members of the household of God. This is a politics of *inclusion* made possible by bringing others to the table in our cities and swamps where decisions are made.

Understanding the regime in the local swamp where you live provides a sturdy craft with which to navigate amid the roots, stumps, and mud. It should serve as a reminder to us all that we are urban citizens who have the obligation not only to participate in local decisions ourselves but also to bring others to participate. Our churches can serve as bridges between people within the community to provide social learning. In this way, decisions are not made in the shadows and the backrooms but with the greater social learning among groups—the result of broader participation in local government.

Carrying the Right Gear:
Every Alligator
is a Politician

by Jim Watkins

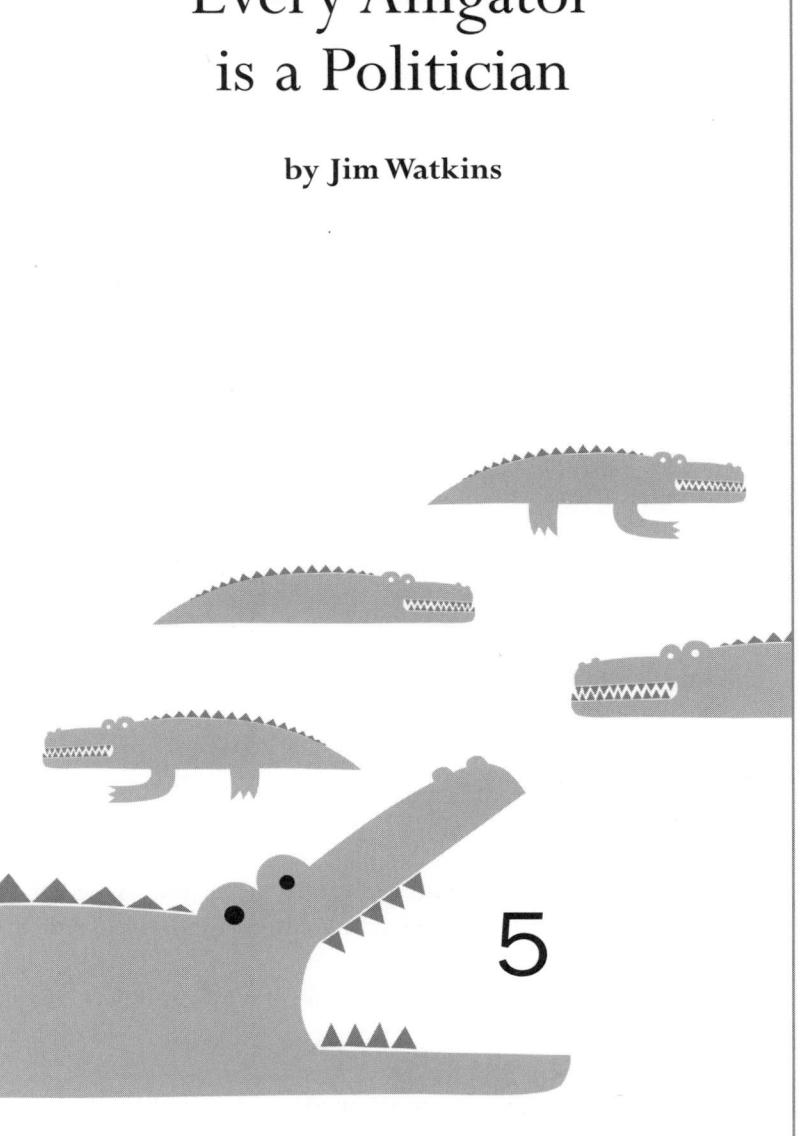

5

Which of the following situations involves politics? Which involves power?

1. Your recent college graduate son wants you to cosign a note with him so that he can buy a brand new car.
2. Your colleague at work with whom you share workspace is a wonderful person to work with except for his messiness, which has now spilled over into your workspace.
3. The worship committee at your church is deciding whether to recommend to the church governing body that choir robes should be green rather than blue.
4. For the third time in a week, your next door neighbor's dog has gotten loose and chased your cat up a tree.
5. The local school board is voting next week on which science curriculum will be taught.
6. Your congregation is trying to get a zoning variance so that it can expand parking.
7. A committee of the state legislature is deciding whether to reduce the state budget deficit by cutting Medicaid payments to nursing homes.
8. Congress and the administration are investigating options to health care reform.

Politics and Power are much maligned and much misunderstood. All the above involve politics and power.

Politics is simply the way people relate to one another to accomplish something. There is politics in our families, schools, neighborhoods, workplaces, and maybe even in our churches. All of us are pretty good politicians. We know how to relate to others in order to get what we want.

Power is the ability to do a particular thing. Look again at the situations described above. Who has the power to cosign, clean up the work area, change the color of the robes, control the dog, choose a curriculum, get a variance, decide on Medicaid payments, develop a national heath care policy? Power moves. People who have power to accomplish something in one arena may not have power in another arena. For example, the local school board does not have the power to decide the color of church choir robes. Like politics, power is involved in all our relationships.

What most people call politics is the public policy process. The public policy process places politics and power, which operate in all human arenas, into the public square where decisions are made for the public good. The public policy process is the way society sets community norms, often through law. What will we teach in our schools? What will our infrastructure (roads, bridges, rail, etc.) look like? What kind of health care will be available, particularly for widows and orphans and the least of these?

Look again at the situations listed above. All involve politics and power. Situations one, two, and three do not involve the public policy process; situations five, six, seven, and eight do involve the public policy process. Situation four could involve the public policy process if your community has a leash law.

Another way of looking at the relationship of politics, power, and the public policy process is reflecting on how church volunteers use time and energy in acts of ministry. (One of the challenges and strengths of doing ministry in and through the church is that most of those who do ministry are volunteers.) These categories are neither good nor bad, right nor wrong. They simply are what they are.

Volunteers engage an issue or community need on a one-to-one basis. An example is serving one night a week in a soup kitchen and befriending a homeless man. This activity improves direct service but has little impact on community norms.

Volunteers create options to a system. An example might be a congregation deciding to build several homes for those in need of affordable housing. This improves direct service and promotes some system change because there are now options available that did not exist before. However, community norms and root causes are still not directly addressed. There will be no long-term change in the system.

Volunteers monitor the system. Monitoring means being present when public policy decisions (community norms for community good) are made and administered and asking questions. "Why?" "What is going on?" An example might be going to the county commission and inquiring about plans for providing affordable housing in the county. This activity provides less direct service than serving in a soup kitchen but has a greater potential for system change as community norms, root causes, and the concept of the common good are addressed in the public square.

Volunteers work for good public policy through advocating for particular legislation. As people use their time and energy to be involved in the public square helping to form legislation for the public good, they may provide less direct service. However, as community norms are changed for the better, as laws are made and enacted, there will be system change. Root causes of human need will be addressed. For example, how do our laws and ordinances embody incentives for building affordable housing?

Finally, volunteers can confront systems in the public square. This does not mean violence. It does mean turning on the spotlight of public opinion. Sometimes, as in the civil rights movement, this activity has the greatest potential for system change. A story on the six o'clock news about the lack of affordable housing helps change the system.

These different ways of doing ministry are not mutually exclusive. One way is not better than another. The construct describes how people do ministry in various ways and what impact their activity has on systems that impact the lives of God's children and creation. People often move back and forth along the continuum according to interest and gifts. That is why the body of Christ has many essential parts. However, any in-depth engagement in ministry in any social justice area will ultimately lead to the public square, where power is used through politics for the common good.

Now that you have all had a chance to talk it over...

Where are most people in the church in terms of their volunteer social-justice activity? Most are engaged in one-to-one activity or in creating options to a system. Again, this is not good or bad, right or wrong. One of the tasks of leadership in the church is to help people engaged in ministry move along the continuum of activity. People who have served in soup kitchens for years and wonder why the lines stay so long can be more effective if they examine their community's provision for low- and moderate-income housing. Volunteers who have worked on housing issues at city hall for years can serve in a soup line every now and then so that the policy they work on has a face.

As persons move from one-to-one and group involvement to monitoring, public policy advocacy, and confrontation, it is important to make sure that they are fed both spiritually and emotionally. One reason that more church folk stay involved with one-to-one activity and creating options is that they are fed from direct contact with those they are helping. It feels good. When persons are engaged in monitoring, advocacy, and confronting, they don't necessarily get the feeding that comes from direct contact. Therefore, it is important for them to get spiritual nourishment in other ways. It is particularly important for persons ministering in the public square to engage in bible study and prayer. It is also critical for those who are being led to find ways of thanking those in public ministry. Someone once said of pastors that if the shepherd is not fed, the shepherd eats the sheep. Sometimes people get frustrated and burned out ministering in the public square because they have not been spiritually and emotionally fed. One way of feeding people engaged in the ministry of using power through politics for the public good is bible study.

We are all familiar with the story of the good Samaritan. Most of us can tell the story by heart. It is told by Jesus in response to the question: Who is my neighbor?

A lone traveler was going up from Jericho to Jerusalem (Jerusalem is literally "up" from Jericho, being at a much higher altitude. It was a perfect route for ambushes from robbers). So it was that this traveler was set upon, beaten, and robbed. Holy people passed the stricken stranger. Finally, a Samaritan, a representative of a group not generally well thought of, stopped and helped. The Samaritan took good care of the wounded man. He put him up at an inn, gave his credit card, so to speak, to the innkeeper, and moved on about his business, promising to pay for everything when he comes back this way. Jesus asked who the neighbor was. The crowd surrounding Jesus responded, "The one who helped." Jesus said, "Go and do likewise." The bottom line of the story is that our neighbors are those in need.

A phrase often overlooked in this favorite and often-preached story is "When I come back this way." That phrase implies that the Samaritan was on that road often. The phrase triggers our imagination. What if, as he traveled the road frequently, the Samaritan found the same situation—someone beaten up and robbed, lying in the ditch beside the road? For awhile he could keep bandaging up victims, putting them on his donkey, and paying for their lodging while they got well. If he continued to do that, he would certainly continue to wear the title "Good Samaritan," but sooner or later, as his personal resources gave out, as his credit card reached its limit, he would have to look for other options. If he did not, then he would have the new title, "Dumb Good Samaritan." In fact, he could write a book, "Charity for Dummies."

In the face of an epidemic of trounced-on travelers, the Samaritan could have organized a buddy system for those on the road. He could have put up warning signs for travelers or called city hall to plead for more and better police coverage in this high crime area. Or perhaps he could have lobbied for stronger laws that would get robbers off the road while simultaneously pursuing a strengthened education system that would give potential robbers other ways of earning a living. He certainly could have told the story to a reporter at the *Jerusalem Journal.* That reporter would then investigate the situation and discover all the other victims and benefactors and tell their stories. A constituency would soon be built to make the road safer.[1]

Let's leap across the centuries and look at a situation not unlike that of the good Samaritan.

The women of First Church were looking for an outreach project. They decided to take gifts and spend time with the residents of Parkview Nursing Home. They contacted the home to arrange to visit once a month on Saturdays. They were all excited when they gathered at the church for their first visit. Carrying the toiletries they had bought and plants they had potted, the women went to Parkview. They quickly got beyond the awkwardness of meeting new people because they were warm and loving women who genuinely cared about the residents. The residents came to look forward to the faithful and happy visits by the women of First Church, and the women came to know them all by name.

On their fifth or sixth visit to the home, one woman resident, Esther Scott (names have been changed) happened to mention to Margaret Brown, the First Churcher who had adopted her as a special friend, that she had recently seen a television news story about a fire in a nursing home and it frightened her. Margaret listened sympathetically and could understand how helpless and vulnerable Mrs. Scott might feel since she was confined to a wheelchair. Mrs. Scott also said it worried her that the aides in the nursing home were often careless with cigarettes.

Margaret tried to put herself in Esther's place. She began to watch the smoking that went on in unauthorized places. She looked carefully at the exits and fire doors. She looked for fire extinguishers and smoke alarms and a sprinkling system. She talked to the other First Church women about Esther's worries and shared her own observations, suggesting the nursing home might not be up to code as far as fire laws were concerned. They all said they didn't know much about the local fire laws.

A few weeks later, Grace Meyers of First Church came away from Parkview and shared a story with the group that another resident had told her. John Wilson had become Grace's friend. He told her that on several occasions staff members stole money from his wallet. At first Grace was not sure whether to believe him, but he was insistent that it was true.

Then one day when Grace came to see John, she noticed a bruise on his face. John appeared very subdued that day and did not want to talk. She asked what had happened to his face. Eventually, she pried the story out of him. He had caught one of the staff members taking money from his dresser drawer; when he had confronted the staff member, the staff member pushed him away, and he had fallen. The staff member threatened him and told him not to tell anyone what had happened. Grace was very upset and confided to the group that she too was frightened of the particular staff person whom John had pointed out to her.

As the weeks went by, troublesome incidents of neglect, abuse, and carelessness surfaced in conversations with other residents of Parkview. Margaret Brown did homework on the fire codes and also asked the director of the home where she could find the fire extinguishers. The director was irritated by Margaret's inquiry and suggested that it might be a good idea for the women of First Church to stop visiting if they were going to make accusations.

Take a moment and reflect on this case study, which is based on a real experience of a local congregation. How would you feel if you were Grace or Margaret? What does the good Samaritan story have to say about this situation? What do you think Grace and Margaret should do? Has anything like this ever happened to you? What does the good Samaritan story have to say to First Church? What should the governing body of First Church do? Should First Church be involved in community issues at all? If so, why? How would you describe what is going on here in terms of politics, power, and the public policy process? What community norms are involved in the situation? Who has the power to address the norms? Who needs to relate to whom in order to access the power to establish norms for the common good?[2]

As people and institutions of faith move into the public square seeking to access power, raising questions about public policy, sometimes a hand is raised and someone asks, "But what about the separation of church and state? After all, religion and politics don't mix, do they?" There is a great deal of confusion about what the separation of church and state means and does not mean.

A working definition of the separation of church and state is: The separation of church and state is the separation of the church as an institution from the state as an institution so that neither controls the other but is not the separation of religious value input from the forming of public policy (setting community norms). In the public square, we set community norms for the common good in areas like care for the elderly, schools, public safety, budget priorities, and environmental protection. Religious value input should be part of the decision-making process. The U.S. representative I worked with asked me during a debate about a human rights issue. "Jim, where are your people on this?" He meant, where is the mainstream church on the issue? Further, he was concerned because he was not hearing from the mainstream church.

Reformer John Calvin said, "No one ought to doubt that civil authority is a calling, not only holy and lawful before God, but also the most sacred and by far the most honorable of all calling in the whole life of mortals."[3] Calvin's thought about the high calling of public service was a natural extension of the Reformed doctrine of the sovereignty of God. God is sovereign over all institutions, church, and state alike, and all institutions are accountable to God.

According to Calvin, the state (government) is a special gift of God, given to assure order, well-being, and relative peace. Believers are to obey the state. Public officials are to govern justly. Because God is at work in all the world, so the church and Christian citizens should be concerned about public matters. Life in the community should reflect, as much as possible, God's will for the world. The church has the responsibility to teach the state about the nature of faith in order that life might be properly ordered. It is the task of the church to advocate and work for changes in the laws that they believe unjust. It is important to remember that Calvin's major theological work, *The Institutes of the Christian Religion,* was addressed to the King of France.[4]

Calvin's thoughts about the role of the state and the responsibility of the Christian in public affairs had an influence on the development of constitutional government, representative government, the right of people to change their government, the need for checks and balances in government, and the separation of civil government from church government.

Calvin's understanding of the nature of humanity made a case for democracy: "The vice and imperfection of men therefore renders it safer and more tolerable for the government to be in the hands of many, that they may afford each other mutual assistance and admonition, and that if any one arrogate to himself more than is right, the many may act as censors and masters to restrain his ambition."[5]

Though Calvin taught that good citizens obeyed civil authority, he also understood that the ultimate allegiance of Christians and the church should be to God. God is sovereign over all earthly powers and requires the ultimate loyalty of the church and individuals. Therefore, if any government requires us to violate our obligations to God, persons of faith should remain loyal, even if that means they will disobey the government. Governments, like people, serve a higher law than themselves. When they do not do so, it is necessary to resist and replace them. American Presbyterian ministers urged resistance to the crown in the 1770s—not on the basis of national feeling, but in the name of the liberty and justice demanded by a sovereign God.

John Witherspoon, the sixth president of Princeton, was the only clergy signer of the Declaration of Independence. Perhaps his most important role in forming a nation was teaching a young student named James Madison. Madison was a major contributor to the U.S. Constitution. The fingerprints of John Calvin, as taught by John Witherspoon, are all over that document. For example, the separation of powers in the Constitution through the establishment of executive, judicial, and legislative branches directly related to Calvin's understanding of humanity. Since human beings often look after their own interests and do no good save by the grace of God, these three branches serve as checks and balances, protection for all human rights.[6]

Like all the reformers, Calvin was a student of Scripture and hoped that all church members would be as well. Those in the

Reformed tradition established schools to make sure that people could read the Bible. If we study the Bible with involvement in public decisions in mind, we find case studies of the involvement of persons of faith in the public square. We can't go to Scripture and find specific instructions about the finer points of health care reform or arms control. But we can look at the whole Bible as the story of God's presence in the creation and find some guides for our life together.

The Old Testament is full of such guides. In Exodus we find the familiar story of a reluctant man prodded by God to enter the public square, confronting public officials as he tried to change public policy. Moses was minding his own business and his father-in-law's sheep when the call came. The official policy of the government of Egypt was to enslave the Israelites. God wanted Moses to be a spokesperson on behalf of the Israelites. Moses was to go to the person who had the power to change the policy of Egypt, the Pharaoh, and challenge him to let the Israelites go free.

Nehemiah is a lesser-known figure from the Old Testament. He moves quickly across the pages of Scripture. Unlike Moses, he is not found in giant sculptures or magnificent paintings. He was never portrayed in glorious Technicolor. And yet, like Moses, Nehemiah heard the call of God to public service in the cries of those who suffered.

The children of Israel, the same people Moses rescued, had not fared well. They had been defeated in war, dragged into exile, and returned to a homeland that had been laid to waste. Nehemiah, comfortably settled as a trusted aide to the King of Persia, heard of the terrible plight of his people from relatives who sought him out. He became convinced that God wanted him to leave his secure position and go to Jerusalem to rebuild the city and restore the confidence of the people. Nehemiah rebuilt a great city and reaffirmed the connection between the interests of Jerusalem and the farmland around it (perhaps one of the first instances of regionalizing as a way of solving problems). Nehemiah also helped the Israelites rediscover their identity as a covenant people.

As part of writing a Bible study on Nehemiah, members of Congress who were active in faith communities were asked to reflect on public service through his eyes. Responses came from Republicans and Democrats. Here is one response:

Nehemiah's challenge was the rebuilding of the walls of Jerusalem. In modern times we may see that challenge as repairing and sustaining the infrastructure of our governments. After I had served my country in the U.S. Marines and the space program, I felt called to take up that larger challenge by running for the United States Senate and serving God by serving my neighbors. I believe that religious faith is something we rely on for guidance everyday wherever we are, and that includes all our activities here on earth, flying in space, serving in public office, or wherever we find ourselves and whatever we are doing. In addition to seeking to know God's will, all of us—especially those in public service—have an obligation to use our talents, our sense of justice and fair play, our own good sense, good will and good judgment, and our love and respect for others in serving one another and governing our personal lives and our nation.[7]

Micah 6:8 is generally recognized as a summary of God's demands as they come to the nation of Israel through the prophets. What is it that God requires of the nation? To do justice, love mercy, and walk humbly with God. This is a statement of specific expectations that call for concrete action in the public square. Walter Brueggeman defines biblical justice as "sorting out what belongs to whom, and giving it back to them."[8] That definition points toward a setting of community norms that upsets an ordering of things Micah sees as unjust. When Micah called the nation to do justice, he did not mean some romantic ideal. He was very specific, as he put a human face on justice. When Micah called for justice, he meant rearranging social structures, the reordering of national priorities. For him that meant canceling debts as called for in the Jubilee Year described in Leviticus 25, redistribution of land and the protection of widows and orphans. Later, canceling debt, rearranging property ownership, and protecting the least of these becomes an important part of the New Testament.

It is clear from the Old Testament that God calls people to be in the public square, raising questions about community norms. The New Testament is also a resource for preaching, teaching, and reflecting on the relationship between church and state.

The model of Jesus and the views of the early Christian community can be useful in sorting out that relationship. But we need to be aware of the challenge of taking issues from the first century and using them in our own time. Again, one important guideline for interpreting Scripture is: What did the passage mean to those who first heard it?

Jesus' parables, sayings, and actions show deep concern for the poor, the least of these, and the stranger, whether or not they belong to the fellowship of believers. Did Jesus call for actions against the government? It is difficult to tell. The cleansing of the Temple is one of Jesus' most public actions, but it is not altogether clear what Jesus is protesting. Often, as in Luke 22:36, 51, two contradictory statements from Jesus are side by side. In the former passage, Jesus urges that the person who has no sword must go and buy one; in the latter, he takes to task those who would fight back.

In the New Testament, then, we find two distinct positions on the relationship between church and state: unquestioned acceptance of ruling authorities and unquestioned resistance to authority. We see both these two positions in Matthew 22:21–22 ("Give to Caesar that which is Caesar's and to God that which is God's"). We could interpret the passage as an instruction to obey the state, the coin and taxes being symbols of obedience. In contrast, the hearer might conclude that since everything ultimately belongs to God and has God's image on it (just as the coin has Caesar's), ultimate allegiance belongs to God. Therefore, they should resist the state.

In translating first-century thought to our time, it is important to remember that these two points of view—unquestioned obedience and unquestioned resistance—presuppose a governmental system against which the community has no power. Those who first heard Scripture did not live in a representative democracy. If you did not agree with Caesar, you did not write him a letter (oh, you might do it one time) or support the other party's candidate in the next election. However, we do live in a representative democracy, formed in part, as we have previously seen, by Reformation thought. How do we make a difference in our representative democracy where we do have power?[9]

How do we access power to help form sound public policy that seeks to make society just, fair, and loving in a way that is pleasing to God? A document from one denomination, "Christian Obedience in a Nuclear Age," offers suggestions.

The primary course in seeking the transformation of political and economic policy is the vigorous and creative use of the ordinary and legal means available to us as citizens of a nation. Many studies across the spectrum of the church show remarkable agreement that neither the corporate structures of individual churches nor the great majority of individual members have yet pursued this strategy in a truly serious and sustained way. The document does not support the formation of a Christian political party or the endorsement of parties or candidates by denominations, but rather supports using the public policy process fully and creatively. Voting in elections is critical, but voting is not enough. Democratic systems offer the possibilities for helping select candidates, for questioning prospective candidates, for participating in campaigns, as well as writing and visiting elected officials. Educating officeholders regarding critical matters, by providing facts and other background material, is another possibility. Finally, there is also the opportunity to stand for public office or to enter government service directly.[10]

Doing ordinary things in extraordinary ways begins with gaining access to elected officials and their staff by building long-term relationships through communicating. Building relationships in the public square is like building relationships in other settings. As human beings, we relate to one another in a variety of ways to accomplish goals. To be human is to be political. Remember, we are all politicians. As we said earlier, politics is everywhere—in our families, schools, neighborhoods, places of work, and, yes, even our churches. Public officials and their staff are just like us. We relate to them the way we relate to others. Political skills are interpersonal skills. Relationships, relationships!

But before we go about building those relationships, we need to know what we want to accomplish. We need to think and act strategically.

Most folks try to be players in the public square by beginning with tactics. Tactics are short-term activities that get you where you want to go. Strategic thinking and acting defines where you want to go. Strategic thinking and acting involves knowing your destination. Tactical thinking tells you how you will get to your destination. Most of us do not start out on a trip unless we know where we are going.

When we get to the edge of town, it makes all the difference in the world whether we are going to the mountains or the beach.

Effective players in the public square know where they want to go. What issue and/or piece of legislation is most important?

Before we start building relationships with public officials and their staff, we also need to know the components of a decision that any public official makes. Envision a pie. One slice of the pie is core value. All public officials have core values. No matter what anybody else says or does, they will not violate their core values. The representative I worked with was an actor. It is not surprising that his core values included protecting the First Amendment right of free speech. Another slice of the pie is "significant others," staff, colleagues, trusted friends, etc. All public officials are highly dependent on information shared by those they trust. All public officials are educated beyond their intelligence. That does not mean they are stupid. It means that they have to know so much about so many things that they can not possibly know about everything they have to vote on. Another slice of the decision pie is special interest groups—the dreaded lobby. If you agree with them, they are an interest group. If you do not agree with them, they are a lobby. There is a place for interest groups in the public policy process. There are groups that do know a lot about particular issues because they deal with those issues everyday. The largest part of the decision pie is constituents. What do my constituents think? Public officials are constantly trying to find out where their constituency is. That makes communicating points of view with public officials critically important.

How do we give input into public decisions? First of all, we need to realize that our task is not to convince public officials. No one has ever been convinced by anyone of anything. People give input to others. That input may be used in helping form a decision, but the decision is internal to the person deciding. Our task is to relate to public officials as effective communicators giving input into public decisions.

All effective communication, whether verbal or written, has two parts. The first part is recognizing where the other person is. The second part is clearly stating where we are. In communicating with others, particularly in stressful situations, we tend to do either the

Sometimes alligators have big decisions to make.

first part or the second part. That tendency is really part of the old flight or fight reaction to stressful situations. Some of us, when threatened or under stress (and communicating with public officials can be both), flee by always recognizing the other's position but never saying where we are. When we do that, we never get anywhere. Others tend to respond by always stating what we want without regard to the other person's point of view. If we keep doing that long enough, we will get into a fight. It does take practice to put the two parts of effective communication together. Theologically, the people we communicate with are children of God and have the right to their opinions. We are also children of God and have the right to our opinion. Remember, our task is not to convince but to communicate.

Being an effective communicator does not mean always getting what we want. Sometimes it means opening up the possibility for compromise. Important public decisions always have multiple points of view represented. We want to make sure that our point of view is represented in the mix.

As we take our political skills into the public square in order to make sure our point of view is represented as decisions are made, we use two forms of communication—direct and indirect.

Direct communication involves letter writing, telephoning, visiting, attending town hall meetings, and so forth. Indirect communication involves writing letters to the editor, submitting op ed pieces to newspapers, calling talk shows, media coverage, communicating with people who know people with connections. Indirect communication helps form the backdrop, the general sense of where the public is on an issue.

The general rule for direct communication is: That which takes the most care and time to do has the greatest impact. In terms of written communication, a well thought-out letter generally has much more impact than a petition with hundreds of signatures. A well-dressed petitioner can stake out a shopping mall in the Midwest on a Saturday morning and get several hundred signatures in favor of saving alligators in Lake Michigan. Receivers of petitions (with the exception of signatures needed to put a referendum on a ballot) will be polite but not swayed. The nagging question is always, "Do these folks really know what they are signing?"

In contrast, a well-written letter shows a public official that the sender really does know what he or she is writing about.

An effective letter to a public official includes:

1. A salutation. Say something nice, even if only to recognize that the official has a tough job.
2. Your credentials. There is no one who is a greater authority on you than you. You are first of all a constituent (which translates into voter). Then you are a parent, student, homemaker, minister, teacher, businessperson, and so on.
3. A message. Clearly state your issue, the reasons for your concern, and what position you would like the official to take on the issue.
4. A request for response. Ask the official to reply. Most people never ask for a reply.

5. A final word of appreciation. Thank the official for the work that she or he is doing.

Effective letters are one page and tightly focused on one issue or piece of legislation. It is generally best not to refer to a group that has asked you to write. Avoid triggered communication. Elected officials are looking for a broad-based consensus among constituents.

Letter writing can be planned and organized in a way that does not seem to be triggered. A letter-writing party is fun. Gather folks for dessert and coffee. Explain the issue at hand. Have plenty of stationery and writing instruments. Encourage participants to write in their own words. Stamp the letters with different stamps. Collect the letters. Over the next week, put the letters in different mailboxes. Lots of letters can be generated without them having a triggered ("someone told me to write") feel.

A visit to a public official has the same flow as a letter. When you greet the public official and/or his or her staff, say something nice. Introduce yourself using the same guidelines as letter writing. You are a constituent (the magic word). You do such and such as an occupation. You are visiting because of your concern about such and such an issue or piece of legislation. Ask the official where she or he stands on the issue or legislation. Thank the official and/or staff for the time spent with you. An optimum number of visitors is three. One person focuses on the official and is the prime spokesperson for the group while another person focuses on staff; the third person acts as timekeeper. Be sensitive to the official's schedule. A visit will probably last no more than fifteen minutes. If the official or the staff person wants to continue the conversation, they will let you know. Nothing will damage your visit more than overstaying your welcome.

Phone calls have the greatest impact if there is a large number of them and if they are made prior to an important decision. It is easier to call than it is to write. Writing is preferable, however, if you have the time.

As noted, most elected officials have certain issues that are so important to them that they will risk their careers for those issues. Most of the time, however, elected officials vote for what they believe is in the best interests of their constituents—the common good. A vote in Congress or at the state house or city hall often means that the official has determined what the majority of his or her constituents want. But, since most constituents never write, call, or visit, officials often rely on indirect communication to get a fix on their constituency. Whatever influences public opinion will ultimately influence public officials.

It is important to get to know persons in the media. Who covers the issues that concern you? Often we send press releases to faceless addresses and wonder why the paper doesn't send a reporter. If we know the reporter, our press releases might find their way to the top of the stack on his or her desk.

The first thing that most elected officials and staff do in the morning is read the paper. A timely letter to the editor can help form opinion. One of the staff persons in our congressional office clipped letters to the editor every morning and placed them in the center of the congressperson's desk.

When you write a letter to the editor, make your opinion clear from the beginning. Don't try to combine opinions of several issues in one letter. Keep sentences, paragraphs, and letters short. The more concise the letter, the more likely it is to be published. Make sure you have all the facts, names, dates, and quotations correct. Cite sources if possible. Don't worry about having to be a professional writer. Your own reasoned judgment communicates better than well-turned phrases. Write about whatever you think is important. Letters can inform, make suggestions, react to news or other letters, critique, and say thank you. As with writing a letter to a public official, say something nice about the paper. Papers perform an important role by encouraging moral discourse.

An often-overlooked form of indirect communication is passing information through those who know the official. If you get to know staff well and are trusted by them, they may tell you who the elected official looks to for advice. Biographies of elected officials are also good leads as to who knows whom. Is the official active in the Scouts or Rotary? Where does he or she go to church? What schools did she or he attend? Get a biography from the official's office.

Another way of indirect communication is looking at the list of people who contribute to the elected official's campaign. For local offices, you can obtain the list of contributors from your county elections office. For statewide and congressional offices, your secretary of state will have a list. Many states and some counties are now computerized so you can go on-line to find out the information. You might be surprised to see who is on the list. You just might know someone who is a contributor.

Those who contribute to an elected official are not buying votes. The cynicism abroad often makes that incorrect assumption. What contributions sometimes do is provide access. Contributions indicate support, and we tend to know those who support us.

After we know why we are advocating, what we are advocating for in the long run, and how to advocate, then we need to make sure we know the lay of the land. Who are the staff persons who work with the officials whose support we seek? All elected officials, whether a county commissioner or a U.S. senator, do two things: They form public policy, and they provide constituency service, helping solve problems with the government. They have a staff that helps them do those two jobs. Some staffs are small. State representatives may have one person who performs both duties. Other staffs are larger. A congressional office may have up to twenty people. Get to know staff!!! Get to know those who relate to the issue and/or agency you are interested in.[11]

There is often a short jump from communicating with public officials to being involved in the election process. My journey toward being senior staff with a U.S. representative began with putting up a yard sign. Persons of faith can be involved in the election process by helping candidates with whom they identify or by running for office.

A friend once described a call as a need the church has and a person's ability to meet that need. If the two meet, that is a call. In election terms, a sense of call can be described as having a fire in your belly. People who decide to run for office have to really want to run. In order to go through what a person goes through in a campaign, running for office requires a steadfastness of purpose forged from an inner desire that pushes a person into the public arena. A candidate simply has to run for office. He or she can do no other.

Often candidates find a place to run by looking at an area of government they have been involved in. One member of a board of education ran for office after she had been involved in the parent/student/teacher association. She came to see that she could make education policy decisions as well as and maybe even better than those she knew on the school board. A county commissioner decided to run after having successfully led neighborhood opposition to a zoning decision.

Sometimes circumstances thrust a candidate onto the public stage. There was a pastor whose parish member won a position as the school board chair for the county. The chair-elect died of a massive heart attack. At the funeral, the pastor was asking the rhetorical question, "Who will replace our friend?" From somewhere the inner voice came to the pastor: "What about me?" Later, friends asked the pastor to consider running, validating the inner call. The pastor won the special election and helped the school board navigate difficult times.[12]

This chapter has made a case for beginning with process and moving to issues. My experience has been that it is important to know why we are doing what we are doing, who we are doing it with, and how we are going to do it before we do it. Therefore, the chapter has included a biblical and theological basis for involvement of persons of faith in the public square. We've also added to our practical political skill bag. Now let us turn to the identification of issues in the public square that merit our attention.

Ted Wardlaw, then pastor at the Central Presbyterian Church in Atlanta and now president of Austin Theological Seminary, addressed the Georgia House of Representatives in the opening devotions. He made the following appeal:

I know a man named Michael who sleeps near my office windows. Once in awhile, we give him new pair of shoes. The only things he owns, aside from the clothes on his back, are a Bible and an Episcopal Book of Common Prayer. Who speaks for that man?

There is a little boy who is cared for during the day by our Child Development Center—the same center that my little two year old attends. This little boy's father and mother got into an argument almost a year ago now, and his father shot his mother and killed her. Later, he shot and killed himself. I heard his story and was tempted to file it away in that bulging file our culture has labeled "Family Violence." We know all the buzzwords: the dissolution of the family, children having children, guns-aren't-the-problem-criminals-are-the-problem. But all those buzzwords, if we aren't careful, can distance us from the people, like that little boy, who are in crisis. I felt those words working on me. So I went down the hall that separates my office from his nursery and visited that little boy. He was asleep in a crib—his face so round and perfect, his eyelashes so long and beautiful, his fingers and toes so delicate. Who speaks now for that little boy?

There's a woman who comes into our building, sometimes, begging. She's mentally ill. When she doesn't take her medicine, she talks to herself. She's not my mother, not your mother, but whoever her relatives are, [they] are long gone. Who speaks for her now?[13]

The church is at its best in the public square when it accesses power on behalf of those who have no voice. I was working for Congress when the world was made aware of the famine in Ethiopia. During a six-month period, our office received about fifty letters asking for the congressman to make U.S. aid available to Ethiopia. During that same six-month period, we got over six hundred letters complaining about airport noise. This is not to say that the people who complained about the airport were wrong or bad. It simply illustrates the point that rarely in the public square do we find persons advocating on behalf of someone else, particularly if that someone else is a child, and a foreign child at that. One of the realities of the U.S. Congress is that assignments on committees that have to do with things like providing foreign aid and caring for children domestically or internationally are not the most popular. This does not mean that representatives and senators do not care about such issues. It simply points to the reality of a representative democracy. Children can't vote, and if it's a foreign child, the child's parents can't vote.

Those who make their voices heard often get policy formed to their liking. The quickest turnaround of policy that I witnessed was the repeal of a provision for catastrophic health care insurance. The Democratic Congress was overwhelmingly in favor of the measure.

It is God who has made us, and not we ourselves.

The Republican president thought it the best thing since sliced bread. The interest groups that represented older people were pleased with the provision. And then the message began to circulate around the country that catastrophic health care would be funded through an additional surtax on older citizens. Within a matter of weeks, each congressional office got over five thousand letters protesting the measure, and it was repealed. It was not the finest hour for Congress or the administration. Certainly those who needed the provision most were not able to express their viewpoint. The point is that in a representative democracy, the squeaky wheel does get the grease.

In order for those who cannot speak or who speak very softly to be heard, people like you and me—persons of faith who are also voters and constituents of public officials—must speak. By speaking,

I'm talking about the sometimes overwhelming work of organizing people, writing letters, visiting representatives, working for candidates, even running for office. With all due respect to my good friend Ted Wardlaw, the members of the Georgia House expected him to say what he said because he is a preacher. Later in that session, the Georgia House voted three to one to allow more people to carry concealed weapons. In my opinion, that policy will orphan more children.

What public officials don't routinely expect is for a broad base of constituents to focus on legislation and say for the children, or the elderly, or the disabled, do this!

How do you choose which issues to work on? The church benefits from the thoughts of others who have also wondered about the relationship between their faith and issues within the public square. One way to choose issues is to see what others are working on and join forces as allies. Violence against women, the environment, a fair tax system, public education, health care, war and peace…. The list goes on and on.

As you choose your issue, remember to focus. One issue or piece of legislation is great. Two issues or pieces of legislation are okay. Three issues or pieces of legislation are so-so. More than that is a disaster. Church folks and others of good will often shotgun issues and therefore are ineffective on any single issue.

Pick issues that can be won and are easily defined. If you cannot explain the issue to the person in the pew, find another issue to work on. That said, faithful following may, at times, require engaging issues that cannot be won in order to bear witness.

At this point, you may be nodding your head in agreement. However, perhaps a question remains. How can I help my congregation get on board? The best way to help congregations become responsible congregations in the public square is through the functional life of the church—education, pastoral care, preaching and worship, and outreach.

Sometimes we wonder why churchgoers in the pew don't get excited about church education offerings that involve the social dimension of faith. We announce the class and assign a book to read and wonder why people aren't breaking down the door to get into the class. The manner in which the subject is presented may be the reason for their unenthusiastic response.

Adults learn what they want to learn and should be partners in the educational process. This is particularly true when the subject matter has the potential for provoking disagreement. As with effective advocacy, effective education begins with relationships, not issues. "Living Faithfully in the Public Square" is designed for an adult church school class. It is based upon a group process that invites all participants to bring their interests and their gifts to the learning table. Recruitment for the suggested class involves piquing curiosity. What is politics? Is power a four-letter word? What goes on behind closed doors? Ground rules are established for discussion. No one will speak twice until everyone has had a chance to speak a first time. We are in the class to listen in order to understand and not refute. Disagreement is regarded as normal. "Weapons will be left at the door"—no name calling. The agenda, which will include guests who are in public service, will be planned by class members.

How do we preach and lead worship about something that may have some controversy attached to it? Embody a respect for differences of opinion and speak in a way that is "peaceable."

Remember, we point to and become part of what God is doing in this world. So the central focus of worship and preaching is God, not us, or an issue. Following my time in Congress I found myself including in the invitation to the Lord's Table, "This is not the Democratic, Republican, Libertarian or Independent table, it is the Table of Jesus."

Be specific and tangible. In prayers don't pray for "all the world's leaders." Pray for public officials by name. Cite newspaper headlines in prayer. Sermon illustrations are concrete. Do your homework. Just because we are religious folk does not mean that we know anything about affordable housing, health care, or the history of Iraq.

Put the pastoral together with the prophetic. Encourage dialogue. Use humor. Laughter is indeed the grace of God and often paves the way for hearing tough things. As a preacher, don't take yourself too seriously. Speak confessionally, not dogmatically. Don't tell people what they ought to think or do. Share your fears, concerns, learning experiences. Share how you see it, not how they should see it.

Remember, no one has ever convinced anyone of anything.

Give people in worship some handle to grab hold of. Share with them how important it is to write that letter, make that visit, learn about that issue, pray about that victim.... One of the definitions of depression is that a person sees no way out. Give the worshiper something to do. Preach and lead worship out of a sense of God's vision for the world. The bottom line is not oughts and shoulds but God's will for creation.

We all live here together.

Pastoral care is not only for individuals but for the congregation and the community. The parish of a pastor is broad and deep. He or she pays regular visits to those in his or her community who make tough public decisions—the mayor, the members of councils, the newspaper editor, the director of the chamber of commerce, the school board chair, etc. The pastor who seeks to be a public as well as a ministerial leader also pays particular attention to those in her or his congregation who serve in elected or appointed public office. The pastor may find himself or herself helping the public official wrestle with tough public issues.

Pastoral counseling may lead to public issues. A family under stress might trace its stress back to economic downturns and the movement of businesses to another state or country.

Hopefully, by now, the importance of any social justice outreach ministry having a public-policy advocacy component is clear. The use of power for the common good is a critical affirmation for those who seek to point to and become part of God's wholeness giving in a broken world. What makes this affirmation so critical is that the common good is often not a consideration, as we have become islands of individualism. We've seen in this chapter that radical individualism is not central to our faith. Rather, from a biblical, historical, and theological point of view, concern for community building is at the heart of what we as believers are called to.

If the imperative is to participate in the process of making policy decisions in the public square, why do so few people get involved? I used to think that if people would do enough Bible study and read John Calvin, they would jump into the public square.

I've changed my mind. I had fallen into the trap that right thinking leads to right acting. Not so. Feelings, rather than thoughts, most often rule our behavior. The answer to equipping church persons to be good citizens in the public square is not simply to teach a course or preach a sermon and wait for people to rush out and write letters to their representatives.

The biggest barrier to getting involved in the public square is fear of the unknown, of making a mistake, of being out of control, of being overwhelmed. Fear is powerful. Fear takes hold when we begin to do something that we have never done before. The only way I know to handle fear associated with doing new things is to begin to do those new things.

In one of my less sane moments, when I was in the army, I volunteered to be a paratrooper. For three weeks we practiced jumping out a door and landing and rolling on the ground until those activities became automatic. I knew all the mechanics of jumping and I wanted to get my wings. But I still had to go out the door. There is no fear like that of leaving the door of a perfectly good airplane!

After my first jump, I asked the jumpmaster, who had made thousands of jumps (including a jump into Normandy during World War II), if a person ever gets over the fear of leaving the door of the airplane. "No," he said, "and if you do, don't jump."

If you and/or the folks you lead in your congregation have never written or visited a public official, the thought of doing so will bring anxiety. If you or someone in your congregation has had a thought about running for office, the anxiety produced by that thought may have pushed the possibility back deep down within you or them. If you have thought about preaching on matters in the public square, perhaps your anxiety has stopped you from tackling the topics. Go on out the door! When you do, you will find that you are not alone.

Alligators in the Swamp: Reflections on Ministry Practice and Leadership

by George B. Thompson, Jr.

6

Our journey through the swamp of church life has kept us busy. We have considered what kind of clothing to wear, wanting to look the part and be ready as we get splashed by alligator activity. We have checked out our maps and made sure that our compass was working so that we don't get lost. We have tried out our boat to ensure that we would be able to get around easily and safely. Finally, we tested our swamp gear to be prepared for whatever the adventure would offer. All of this preparation has helped us appreciate what we would discover: That swamps are big; they sometimes look beautiful, but they also can be dangerous. Swamps have a power all their own.

It remains, then, in this chapter to ruminate upon this journey through church and power that this book invites. What does power look and feel like from the four vantage points presented here? How might congregations think, decide, and act differently because of them? What particular themes and challenges face those in the church who seek to lead, rather than simply to flex their alligator muscles? How can the church's theological task express this view of power in ways that move beyond mere doctrinal rhetoric? Can all God's creatures live in the swamp without constantly muddying up the waters?

In this chapter we will explore and suggest directions in response to these questions. Our beginning point will be a review of main themes and points from each of the central chapters. It also seems important to consider a few other themes that have been implied in this discussion of power: the effect of change, the potential for abuse of power, religious practices, and the nature of leadership. Ultimately, the most critical theme could be that of how power is exercised faithfully in ways that promote leadership. Leadership and power are not the same thing, although leadership does not occur without power in play. Learning the difference becomes one of the points of wisdom for being able to lead.

Summaries

We have explored in this book four perspectives on power, four slices of the complex human realities out of which power emerges and acts. These four approaches could have been treated in any order, but we began with self for a reason that might be obvious. It is that the historical development of American society regards personal human integrity and agency to an extent not previously experienced. In America the individual tends to be number one. Our views of community and responsibility have become heavily shaped by individualism. To talk of power in an American context, then, means to address human selfhood up-front and early. In other parts of the world, where human selfhood is viewed tightly in relation to family, tribe, or community, we would begin a discussion of power elsewhere, such as in culture. In the context of the American cultural influence, it makes sense to start with self. Let us begin there, as we review the four.

Self and power

Chapter two discusses self-understanding primarily from perspectives that traditionally have been kept on society's margins. By paying attention to looking at what it is like to live in society as a woman, to deal with her self, encourages all of us—both females and males—to face two basic realities: One, forces in our world silence certain voices in order to favor others; and two, what it is like to find one's own self as one lives on the edge. Chapter two emphasizes that voicelessness occurs not just for women but also because of racial and ethnic heritage. People who are not "white" (as American society has defined it) historically have had little opportunity in America for voice and power. The marginality that took away their voice was not by their choice; it was given to them. We explored in chapter two how this social construction affects the development of self. No wonder, then, that gangs remain a consistent feature of American urban life. A sense of personal integrity—self-worth—is deeply tied to being part of a community that permits you to exercise some power.

Squirming: The Shoe Fits

For perhaps most readers, our consideration of self from the margins creates a degree of discomfort that attends. If we already have been there, we are reminded of the ways in which forced marginality confines and even harms us. If we rarely have been conscious of marginality in our own lives, reading about it could trigger feelings of denial and defense. As was stated, men and boys need to be freed from the harmful confines of certain limiting images of the male self. The female images of struggle with identity and self that were shared in chapter two need not be directed only to women. Power in a society has more chance of being used for good when it is widely, not narrowly, available.

Fear Factor

Less explicit in chapter two, but just as relevant to any discussion of power, is the importance of coming to grips with one's own fear. One of the most significant experiences that affects the nature and use of power is that of fear. Virtually everyone knows what it is like to be afraid—of losing a job, of a son or daughter being seriously hurt, of making a fool of one's self, of seeking to find a way to speak for yourself, of failing to reach a treasured goal, of friends or colleagues shunning you, of dying alone. Learning to deal with fear is one of life's biggest challenges. As a pastor, I have gone through some major bouts with fear, primarily around employment. When the work situation became difficult and appeared intractable, I think that my biggest fear was how I would be able to support myself and my family. John Harris notes how this dependence upon the congregation for financial well-being complicates the pastor's role and behavior.[1] A threat to a pastor's economic security surely triggers a well-founded fear.

Fear Out of Control

Regardless of the source of the fear, people who are afraid risk engaging power inappropriately. Think again of the four PACE styles and how each one reacts to negative stress. A Conducting-style pastor might seek to attack the perceived source of the fear itself. This could take the form of devising a way to thwart a church member's particular action. This kind of strategy could lead to tension and outright conflict in the congregation. A pastor in Predicting-style excess due to fear might withdraw, keeping to her- or himself, saying little in the church's public arena, trying to figure out what to do next. This kind of strategy could leave the pastor vulnerable to charges of incompetence, or to becoming a victim of church members' action, thus rendering him or her fairly powerless. A third fearful pastor could function out of the Attending style in stress and fear. He or she would avoid situations that trigger the fear, trying to placate anyone perceived as invested in the fear-related dynamics. This kind of strategy could leave the pastor smiling on the outside but a nervous wreck on the inside. Church members might wonder about promises made by the pastor to one group over another. A fourth fearful pastor could operate out of the excesses of the Excelling Style. She or he would be in danger of lashing out at certain members, accusing them of undermining the pastor's authority, of doing something wrong, or even of abandoning the faith. This kind of strategy could polarize the congregation, triggering attempts by factions to win the contest.[2]

Any of these styles of response to fear eventually could hurt both the pastor and the congregation. Fear throws power off, sending it in less useful—and sometimes destructive—directions. *The swamp does not benefit when the alligators are afraid of something.* A pastor who has not learned to manage her or his fear will not use power well and is not ready to lead.[3] He or she might be able to accomplish things, even with good intentions for the congregation. The scepter of fear, however, makes leadership difficult to undertake.

Self and Leading

What, then, might this approach to self and power contribute to the ability to lead? In our view, it is the absolute starting point. A community or group that experiences leadership depends upon at least one person who can keep her- or himself managed and focused on the situation, rather than one's self. Keeping out of the way of the need at hand is a skill effectively exercised by one who has gotten their act together by first "working on their own stuff." A person who helps a group accomplish something unexpected might be called a hero; the person who can help the group sustain such constructive movement over time is leading. Whether the same person can move them from a moment of achievement to a style of learning and growing will depend initially upon that person's own inner development.

I can look back now at moments in my pastoral ministry and realize how unprepared I was to manage my own anxiety. No wonder I didn't know what to do with the church! No wonder, too, that opportunities to lead vaporized before us—and neither I nor the church members realized it. As the years went by, I eventually got a grip on those issues inside myself. Now I am much more aware of who I am, of how I go about things, and of what I bring to the table. This means that I am more conscious and poised about how I can engage power. *It also means that I am less threatened when I realize that traditionally silenced voices in my midst need to be heard.* In a context that is both Christian and democratic in its espoused values, the power of self is not an end in itself. It contributes to the well-being of community—in other words, it learns how to lead.

Culture and Power

Growing self-awareness and self-management ideally lead a person to improved insights about their place in the world.[4] Chapter three's approach to understanding "place in the world" uses a fairly novel framework from culture. Admittedly, the densest of the book's chapters in terms of sheer conceptual material, chapter three provides a view of the intricacies of human community that is wide-ranging. It uses watery metaphors both of swamp and of flowing streams to depict culture's multifaceted characteristics. We viewed the cultural swamp in three levels: from up on the shore, in the water, and down in the mud. These levels help us distinguish cultural categories that are related to each other but should not be confused. Furthermore, sources of content in all three levels can and do arise from the swamp's relationship to sources of water (read "culture") that flow through it from other places. Out of this double water image emerges a rich picture of church life, one that accounts for much more than many other analytical models. What we see in the church's swamp is not necessarily bad or wrong; after all, swamps are here for a reason! This means, for one thing, that the question of whether the power of this or that congregation's culture is good must be suspended until a careful analysis is done.

Self, Culture, and Power

From the vantage point of chapter two, chapter three argues that the self always is embedded in some kind of community. Self always is influenced by streams of culture that flow all around it and through it. Here the limitations of the myth of American individualism begin to be exposed. No one is an island, cut off from the effects of other individuals, from community practices and beliefs, from networks of relationships and influences, from having to take into account some degree of reliance upon society. In the language of this book, one of the most helpful ways to understand power is through a social category such as culture. Being human is not just about being an individual; it is also about being heavily influenced by complex factors in society.

The power that an alligator exercises, then, always exists in relation to the particular dynamics of the culture in that alligator's swamp. Elsewhere I have talked about the danger of pastors who enter a new parish, having experienced comfortable achievements in a prior parish.[5] The danger rests in supposing that stuff on the shore in the new parish's swamp is tied to the same stuff as in the mud of the previous parish's swamp. Some of these connections might be similar, but others will not be since they have their own idiosyncratic histories. When a pastor misjudges the culture, she or he also misjudges how that congregation's power is available and utilized. Then that pastor ends up feeling less like an alligator and more like the alligator's lunch!

Alligators do not live by bread alone,...

Culture and Leading

What does this approach to culture and power contribute to the ability to lead? Without the capacity for reading the invisible but undeniable effects of the particular swamp's mud, a pastor is vulnerable without even knowing it. Yes, there always will be power in the congregation, but *you can't read what is in the mud if you get stuck in it.* Just as one who aspires to lead must get their act together, so also must they be willing and able to learn what is going on here. This means paying attention, not merely to what is on the shore (the many particular details of the congregation itself) but also to clues about what is hidden in the mud (deep, unconscious beliefs about the way things are). Statistical information can be very misleading! The big question that needs to be explored is, "What does all of this stand for, in this church?" Answers to this need to emerge before any leading can happen.

Leadership is a topic that has received significant attention in research and publication in the last several years.[6] I agree with Lovett Weems on the heart of leadership, which is that it centers upon vision.[7] Vision gets a lot of attention these days, but it often is poorly understood. Vision is not something specific, such as starting a new outreach ministry or constructing a recreation center. These are projects that hopefully fulfill the congregation's stated *mission.* What drives any mission, however, is that picture of the congregation's future with God, its sense of being led to something that is not quite yet. This is *vision,* and claiming a strong vision is the only way that a congregation can fulfill its calling from God. A pastor who learns how to work with her or his congregation's culture is in a better position to help that church see its vision and follow it. Then that pastor is leading.[8]

Regime and Power

One particular form of power in the social realm is the kind in which various groups and networks within a community negotiate with one another on decisions about property, ordinances, governance, municipal spending, and so on. As we saw in chapter four, regime politics might appear to be dominated by one group, such as a downtown business elite. The privileged few alligators who can afford the money and time to play at the local country club often appear to "run everything." Dr. Newman's chapter argues that the power dynamics of any city usually are not as one-sided as all that. Government officials pursue purposes that overlap business interests but not completely. Neighborhood and other groups with their own particular interests will offer yet further goals, at first glance being at odds with government or business (e.g., historic preservation, environmental justice, affordable housing, social services, etc.). Regime politics is a theory that describes what happens when these various groups and concerns meet in the public arena over specific decisions.

"Be Wise as Serpents"

For many pastors, talk of public phenomena in terms of regime politics connotes negative images of church involvement. I am reminded of a seminary colleague of mine from a southern state whose comment first introduced me to something that I had observed even in my home town. Albert's father was a committed Christian and an elected state official; Albert himself was active on campus in governance activities. Yet, he grinned with a knowing look when he said that churches in his home state wanted their pastors to stick to preaching and not get into "meddlin'." This attitude is still common today, particularly in Christian traditions that grew out of working-class or other marginalized sectors of their society.

As a description of one kind of human power, regime politics provides religious communities with a way to analyze what goes on immediately around them. Regime politics by itself does not offer judgment as to whether the actions of those that it analyzes are good or bad. That is a judgment based on ethical standards, often grounded (sometimes distantly) in theology. Because our world is becoming increasingly complex, it is very important for churches—especially their pastors—to be street-smart about the larger swamp in which they sit. Sometimes, it is appropriate for religious voices to speak out against action in the public arena that violates a Christian understanding of the purposes of God on Earth. At the same time, however, this is a role that easily could appear priggish and self-righteous.

Dr. Newman's chapter offers a perspective that justifies church participation in public issues that matter, not just the "moral" ones. Like the historical practice of the New England town meeting, a regime that hears from all the community's voices will more likely fulfill the kind of conciliatory function that the apostle Paul imagined for the fledgling Christian community (2 Corinthians 5:16–20). *There are alligators everywhere in the swamp; they need to learn how to get along with each other and with all the other creatures.*

Regime and Leading

How can an understanding of regime politics help pastors be leaders? What does regime politics contribute to the ability to lead? For one thing, it offers a drop-dead serious look at the way things get done in your community. You might not like what you see. You might believe that it needs to change. How will such change take place? By a ranting preacher organizing a rally, calling the practice in question an evil incarnate? Probably not. Regime politics is one conceptual tool that can help pastors follow Jesus' admonition to "be wise as serpents" (Matthew 10:16). Snakes live in the swamp, too. They know how to get around, both on the shore and in the water. They know how to take care of themselves. They harbor no illusions about the other creatures and their power to do what they want. Pastors who pay attention to the larger swamp of the congregation's community are better prepared to lead it in all kinds of ways.

Advocacy and Power

Thematic relationships between chapters 4 and 5, about the exercise of power, should be evident. Rather than concentrating on descriptive matters, Dr. Watkins takes the next step by discussing a number of ways that people can create and utilize power for the common good. Through astute building of relationships, linking with common interests, and other strategies, Christians can fulfill an often-neglected part of their vocation: that of the public arena. Dr. Newman's comments about Calvin's theology of public life are elaborated in chapter 5. Both Scripture and Christian tradition provide foundations for public participation. This chapter contains plenty of practical advice on a variety of public advocacy topics. *In order for the swamp to be good for every species of creature, everybody needs a chance to be an alligator.*

Church and State

One of the points that Dr. Watkins makes is one that is often misunderstood. The notion of the separation of church and state often has been interpreted by churches as meaning that the church has no business being involved with matters of government. Historically speaking, this view is not accurate. Those who framed the U.S. Constitution sought to prevent what was common in Europe at the end of the eighteenth century, namely, each nation-state having one official church. They wanted a government free from the dictates and maneuverings of a religious body (remember Oliver Cromwell and Puritan England). The new United States would not be Anglican or Presbyterian or any other denomination or religion; it would "disestablish" religion from the state. This meant that bishops or other heads of denominations had no official state capacity and, therefore, no authority outside of their particular denominations.[9]

In spite of this particular history and purpose, the term "separation of church and state" continues to be construed much more broadly. Even certain well-meaning Christians have promoted a complete division between what churches do and what government does. Watkins has argued in his chapter that this division is ill-guided. There are sound theological arguments to promote Christian participation in government as well as historical evidence of its positive effectiveness. There is plenty of power waiting to be exercised in the public arena. If we can imagine an ostrich in the swamp, we would say that *the ostrich needs to get its head out of the water and pay attention—to the alligators!*

Advocacy is Leading

What does public policy advocacy have to do with leading? Clearly, this kind of ministry deals with "power brokering," that is, with people and processes intended to make certain things possible and other things not possible in the wider community. If the United States was a monarchy or dictatorship, the very notion of average citizens being involved in the public sphere would be ludicrous, if not downright dangerous. Since, however, the U.S. is structured on principles of representative government, citizen participation is the backbone of what makes American life distinctive.

In other words, some of the sayings in the water of the American macrocultural swamp assert a place for any citizen to speak and act on matters of legislation. Christians who help persuade law-making decisions toward the goal of a more just society have a chance to lead. Christians can vote on ballot initiatives, put election signs in their yard, campaign for a candidate, or even run for office. Power is always at stake whenever laws or governmental budgets are being made. *The life of any one congregation is played out within the larger swamp around it.* Seeking to engage power for the good of others is an act of leadership.

Abuse of Power

As we noted at the beginning of this book, many religious people find it uncomfortable to speak about power. For Christians, a pietistic image of "Gentle Jesus, meek and mild" leaves no room for seeing authentic faith being anything but submissive. Surely, yielding to the will of God precludes any exercise of power beyond giving up any desire to use it. Otherwise, so this common line of thought runs, power becomes a tool of sin, unfit for gospel work.

"Innocent as Doves"

Attitudes like this one, earnest as they are, nonetheless beg the question that we have sought to address throughout this book. Once we acknowledge that life together involves power, a more fitting question has to do with its use, its engagement. How can Christians participate in power, with faith, integrity, and constructive results? Framing the matter in this way helps us to deal with the negative elements of power in a more realistic way. In other words, if power by nature is not necessarily evil, how do we interpret what is power's misuse? It is all too easy, tragically, to point to incidents of power abuse, even in the church.

Society's willingness in recent years to listen to victims of clergy sexual misconduct simultaneously illustrates and confuses the question of religion and power. Sexual misconduct illustrates all too evidently that church power does get abused, that people are hurt seriously, that institutions are complicit in hiding these violations of human dignity. As devastating as this phenomenon has been, however, we cannot allow one form of power abuse to cloud a complex issue. With limited space available to consider this matter, let us ponder some insights about abuse of power that are suggested by the chapters in this book.

Insights about Abuse

First, we already have implied that power and sin should not be correlated absolutely. The Christian doctrine of original sin suggests that our fallen human nature is most prone to behavior that harms others. It is the sinfulness of human nature, not human relationships themselves, that opens the way to abuse of power. This is a "baby and bathwater" point that needs to be kept clear.

Similarly, we also must distinguish between office and the person filling the office. In the thinking of pastors and congregations, this second insight often—if not commonly—becomes blurred. The pastoral office describes an element of the congregation as an institution. This office is not completely identical with the person who fills it. One reason that persons who fill pastoral roles traditionally have been held to a higher standard is a recognition within the church that the office carries authority that can be used in powerful ways. A pastor's own sense of power as a human being might or might not correlate favorably toward the expectations of the church for what a pastor does in the pastoral role.

Mentioning a pastor's sense of power leads us to the third insight. It is that those who exercise power from an authoritative role (such as pastor) need to be healthy individuals. In the language of this book, pastors must be aware enough to manage themselves and relationships called for by the pastoral role. Not only must pastors find their own voice, they must know how to use it. Pastors who lack sufficient awareness and discipline are those most likely to blur lines between "who I am" and "what pastors do." They are susceptible to stepping over boundaries and abusing power. They are less able to lead.

A fourth insight about abuse, related to the third one, is that it can be driven by more than one cause. Probably the most common stimulus for abuse is fear. People who are afraid that they are going to lose something that they cherish are susceptible to abusing power. Not everything in life is worth fighting over to the death—but try telling that to someone who is afraid. Yet, not everyone who fears acts out of that fear. Many people also believe that they can do nothing about the situation. Often people who use the Attending and Predicting styles in distress become passive players when power is at stake. In contrast, those with a strong desire to see something happen often operate with the Conducting and Excelling styles. The Conducting style in distress will push the person who uses it to be in control. The Excelling style in distress will push the person who uses it to make things right, however she or he perceives "right."

Regardless of the nature of the threat that is perceived, power is likely to be misused if those involved treat the situation only on the surface. In cultural terms, what is in the bottom of the mud of our swamp? What are those deep, mostly unspoken beliefs about life that appear to be threatened? Learning to identify the deeper dimensions of the situation is the key to managing fear and thus of avoiding abuse of power.

Dimensions of Abuse

So far we have spoken about power and abuse in only general terms. Our discussion in the book allows us to recognize that abuse of power can occur in a number of ways. Sexual misconduct is today's most flagrant form of *pastor-to-person* abuse of power. There are other forms, too. I remember one Sunday morning, setting up an adult study class down the hall from the pastor's study. I knew that one of the committee chairpersons was meeting with the pastor there for a few minutes, before morning activities were underway. Suddenly, I heard a loud, shrill voice. It sounded like the pastor's, and I wondered what was going on. I stuck my head out the door and looked down the hall just in time to see the committee chair walk decisively out the door of the pastor's office. She always had been a cheerful, upbeat person, but the look on her face at that moment said otherwise. My pastoral colleague had yelled at her! He had misused the authority of his office; he had allowed his own anxiety about a situation to overcome better judgment. His inability to discipline himself in that moment led to an abuse of power.

Let us look at a somewhat reverse church situation to identify another potential form of power abuse. This one, based on my pastoral and seminary experience, is on the rise, as increasing numbers of declining congregations with quiet desperation seek a new pastor to save them. A *subgroup-to-pastor* abuse dynamic gets set up when persons who represent the dominant subculture of a struggling church advocate an energetic pastoral candidate who is ready to attract new members. In many cases, that new pastor indeed brings new members to this old church, which is set in its ways. To make matters worse, the new pastor introduces new music in worship, adds banners in the sanctuary, participates in youth activities, and gives the new members positions with responsibility. Some of the longtime members realize that this is not what they wanted (which is an irrational belief, since the only way for a church to perpetuate itself is through younger persons replacing old members as they die off)!! So they use the power of their longevity and loyalty to force the pastor to quit. This scenario is not rare; it illustrates the reality of power being abused, not just by pastors, but against them as well.

Sometimes church power abuse occurs *between groups* of members. Such scenarios are more likely to occur in younger churches than in well-established ones. Newer congregations are still discovering what works, what they prefer, how things will be done, and so on. Therefore, they are still negotiating how power will be exercised, by whom, etc. Conflict in young congregations does not automatically lead to abuse of power, but remember original sin! Often a split results, with both remnants subsequently "learning" that bad behavior is acceptable under certain circumstances. In older congregations, the group-to-group conflicts often happen between an established subgroup and a new one. Because the longtime members have more knowledge of the church and more cultural capital than newer members, they believe "deep in the mud" that they have a right to get what they want.[10] This makes the dominant subculture of a church more susceptible to do whatever it takes to maintain control. "Whatever it takes" easily becomes a recipe for abuse of power.

Levels of Response

Let us now consider the problem of abuse of power with the four dimensions laid out in this book. How does one avoid abusing power? It has been implied already that *the key is in self-awareness, discipline, and comfort with one's own voice.* This key might seem obvious or a retread of something that you knew already, yet it strikes me as still highly germane. Know yourself, train yourself, and speak out of self. These three tidbits of advice will go a long way in helping you deal with power, even if you daily face legacies of domination that still exist in our country.

How can an understanding of cultural complexity help you use power appropriately? As has been stated more than once already, *the key rests in what is in the mud,* not on the shore or floating in the water of your church's (or other organization's) swamp. As a newcomer to any situation or organization, you cannot know what is in the bottom of that swamp. While you can become adept at making good guesses, you will need to rely on insiders to name those deeper dimensions.[11] If you are a longtime member or pastor of a particular congregation, you have become enculturated fully into the beliefs in the mud so that you don't think about them. This puts you in danger of abusing power by defending what you are not easily able to articulate. It is important to your proclamation of the Gospel that you create a congregation that believes deeply in not abusing power. In order to do that, your congregation periodically needs to explore its own swamp. Which elements of your church's life are on the shore—worship, facilities, etc.? Which float in the water—sayings that the church uses? Most importantly, what is down in the mud, and how are the other two layers of the swamp linked to things in that mud? The more honest you are in exploring these questions, the less likely your church will abuse power.

How can an understanding of regime politics help a church or pastor face use of power in public? For one thing, it reminds us that

You just might be surprised sometimes about who has power.

Alligators in the Swamp

anyone who wants to get into the public arena needs to put in the time. Players in the regime know each other and how they operate. They don't necessarily like each other, but they come to know what to expect. A pastor or church needs to realize that all of the other players in the regime are *encultured into various confluences* of the mesocultures around you and the microculture of your community. All of those cultures have things lodged down in their respective mud bottoms, and those various items do not always flow together. Sometimes they create logjams. The regime reminds us that culture is very complicated, as is the power it generates. Allow yourself time to enter that world.

Finally, the logical consequence of entering the public world is to deal with potential abuse of policy work. Laws, regulations, ordinances, and budgets all work most readily at the level of the swamp's shore and water. Effectiveness of such public policies depends in large measure upon what is down in the mud of the many cultures flowing in and through the public arena. American society is increasingly diversifying, which stirs up the mud in the public's complex culture. Idealistic persons of faith need to realize that you can't legislate morality. Policy work ultimately must go hand in hand with other ways to make change and use power with integrity.

Power and Change

This book seeks to offer its readers new ways to look at power. Many common notions about power, even among church people, are inaccurate or not helpful. We have tried to identify some of these inaccuracies. One of those that probably needs explicit attention is that of power and change. When I was a young pastor, I remember thinking that the notion of change seemed abhorrent in many churches that I knew. It was almost like using a vulgarity in front of your elders! In my youthful enthusiasm, I often could see things that needed changing if that congregation ever were to move out of its malaise. Early on, however, I decided that I needed to talk about change while avoiding use of the term itself. Otherwise, church members—even the elected officers—tended to feel threatened by what I thought were helpful suggestions.

Most of us who remember the civil rights movement, Vietnam, and Woodstock are keenly aware that the world in which we live continues to change. These changes are technological, political, economic, social, cultural, and you name it. Enough has been written for church audiences to make this point persuasive.[12] We live in a world that is constantly in flux—whether we like it, understand it, or do anything about it. What we often don't realize consciously, even in the midst of experiencing change, is that power often changes, too. Structures of all kinds, as well as deep cultural assumptions, can and do change, usually slowly, but often inexorably.

Change and Conflict

Consider, for instance, the common experience of longtime church members dealing with an influx of new members. At one level, the longtimers welcome the contributions of the newcomers, who provide financial support, participation, and some reassurance of continuity. At another level, new people bring new ideas and practices that often are perceived by longtimers as threatening. Newcomers can be very surprised that their participation leads to episodes of unexpected resistance. Anxiety and resistance occur not only within individuals; they also arise among groups, such as the subculture constituted by a church's longtime members. Chapter 3, on culture, helps us realize that change eventually affects the church's culture. The mud at the bottom of every church's swamp has to adjust when streams of culture bring new stuff and new sayings. Yet culture's natural tendency is to resist since culture by nature is necessary for group stability.

Awareness of these qualities of culture helps us, then, to recognize relationships in churches between power and conflict. If change indeed is inevitable in today's world, and if culture resists change, how can conflict be treated? How and where does power perform? One way to understand conflict is to say that it begins to emerge at those points within the congregation where the use of power is being contested. Yet the matter goes even deeper. Power becomes contested when different groups within the church cling to different submerged beliefs in the mud. Newcomers bring their own cultural mud with them, which does not contain all the same elements as the mud of the church that they have joined. If the discussion about the stuff or the sayings never goes into the mud, the contest becomes a confrontation, and the goal becomes one of using your power to overcome the other group's power.

Change and Context

All too often, and all too tragically, the scenario of congregational conflict and power-playing runs its course. This means that the deeper question, the one that finally makes the difference to the church's future, is not addressed. That question has to do with change for the sake of staying strong in Gospel witness. All too often, conflict in the congregation masks a more fundamental matter of change—namely, that of the *congregation's context.* Newcomers arriving in the church can mean that the neighborhood or town is changing demographically. Perhaps new subdivisions are being built, or old houses are being renovated. A new employer might have moved to town or an old one closed up. There are many factors outside of a congregation that can affect directly who is or becomes part of the church. How well does the congregation pay attention? How has it experienced power up to that point? What is shifting in the dynamics of power? Some persons and/or groups will gain opportunities while others will lose them. We cannot assume that "they" always will have power.

Change occurring around a congregation spells change within it. Eventually, a church changes when its context becomes very different than it used to be. If a church tries to behave as though the change were not occurring, it gradually will lose whatever position of power that it had in its community. Since human communities by nature have power in their midst, power shifts when change happens. Thousands of such stories have been told, often painfully, about churches who cannot adjust their vision when things around them change.[13]

Changing context and conflict are common but also frequently misinterpreted. On the surface, it becomes clear that goals between, say, new neighbors and old congregation differ. "Old guard" subcultures, whether in the neighborhood or the church, tend to want to maintain power, which ends up meaning that they assert it against others. From a cultural standpoint, conflicts rarely deal with the fundamental issue. By squabbling over the stuff that is on the swamp's shoreline, and defending this or that bit of stuff with sayings floating around in the swamp's water, conflict contestants more often than not miss the boat—or, as we should say, the mud.

Change triggers a deep but usually unexamined sense that "we are different," that the deep beliefs in the muds of our respective cultures do not match up. This common phenomenon occurs every time a new ethnic group begins to move into an established neighborhood. Most people assume that the obvious differences make identification of common interests and concerns irrelevant.

The authors of this book are hoping to convince you otherwise. It is possible—yes, even necessary—for different groups in church or community to live together. We cannot expect that these respective cultural muds will be identical; indeed, we know from the stuff on the different shores that they will not be so. Yet confluence theory (chapter 3) also implies that finding overlapping cultural strengths is possible. These strengths can create a common foundation for the new community and thus for appropriate exercise of power.

Power Analysis

In other words, effective engagement of power during change first calls for analysis and understanding. Anyone who aspires to lead in a context of change, at whatever level, needs to be willing to learn about changes in the swamp first. More specifically, she or he should strive to discern links between the stuff on the shoreline and that to which it is connected down in the mud. *One of the first lessons of leading through a conflict is that "the issue" is not the issue*—in spite of what people are feeling and saying.

If change remains, it threatens and changes power. Because culture is a conserving mechanism, lasting change means that some things in the swamp's mud disappear and some new ones appear. That process is not an easy or quick one, however; it actually can take several years to accomplish. Anyone who is in the change business needs to understand the power of cultural resistance and be prepared for dealing with change over the long haul.[14]

Religious Practices

What might it look like for people of faith to take power seriously? As we ponder everything that is written in this book, we can detect hints for religious practice. These hints include specific ideas not only for individual persons but also for groups in the congregation, as well as the congregation as a whole.

Of Persons

It should be very evident by now that anyone who seeks to engage power for good must be very aware of and *honest with* themselves. Religious people can be self-deceived! It happens all too frequently. Many spiritual disciplines across the ages call for this kind of self-awareness in order to keep the soul receptive to the truth about itself. Especially where power is concerned, the human heart is challenged virtually daily to be aware of its desires and motives.

More specifically, one could choose as a devotional theme for a period of time (say, during Lent) to reflect on the theme of power. Bible readings, movies, devotional books, newspaper, and other literature all could provide sources of insight for spiritual rumination. Journal entries about one's own feelings concerning power would help one become clearer about inherited beliefs and fears.

Another way for an individual believer to grow in their own understanding of power is to observe the world around you from day to day. Where do you see power in action? Who has it and how did they get it? Who is being excluded from power and why? What biblical or theological resources do you think speak to any particular dynamic of power that you witness? Just as importantly, ask yourself, "How do I experience and not experience power in my life?" Living with questions like these will sensitize you to power in all of its intricacies. The more that you know about power, the wiser you can be as you seek to engage it.

Of Congregations

One of the quickest ways for a congregation to get in touch with the power in its midst is to look at its polity, *its forms of authority.* What does your denominational tradition require of the pastoral office? In the congregation's governing board? What are the elected and appointed positions and their functions? Remember that these offices and structures and formal designations might not be followed to the letter. What might account for lines and processes of authority not being used in your church? In many cases, the answer will be that the congregation's culture has developed other practices based upon idiosyncrasies within that church's history. Those idiosyncrasies hold key clues to your church's power.

A congregation that is motivated to be faithful in its use of power might decide to *study the Bible.* It would be more fruitful, however, to avoid the predictable pious pattern of studying God's power. Such an inquiry could become so abstract and idealistic that it fails to inform about power in God's world. Instead, use the study to explore together what power looks like from the vantage point of Scripture's human characters. How did Rebekah, Moses, Ruth, David, Jeremiah, Jesus, and Paul experience power? What kinds of power did they utilize, with what effect? How did they attribute their actions to the purposes of God? By asking questions like these in a Bible study, without the prejudice of easy Sunday school answers, your study group could discover many useful insights.

Beyond formal structure and Bible study, a group on behalf of the congregation also could move into an *examination of the culture* itself. First, what is the stuff on the shore of your church's swamp? Next, what floats in the water as expressions of value used to explain what is on the shore? Most importantly, what do answers to the first two questions leave unanswered? In other words, what is down in the mud that needs to be uncovered enough to identify the cultural foundations of your church? How much consistency is there between the layers of your swamp? *The keys to the church's power lay in the mud.*

Congregational self-examination can focus also upon its place within your community. What forms of power exist beyond your walls? How are they exercised? How is your church related to those outside forms of power? Answers to the questions could help the church be more honest about how people outside your church perceive it. Some of what you discover might not be flattering, but it could stimulate a new conversation about your mission.

One last suggestion for congregational practice with power has to do with the *ministry of education*. What are you teaching children about power? Is everything that they learn about it implicit, picked up through observation rather than teaching? How consistent is the congregation? In other words, if Jesus is presented as meek and mild, how does the church behave when there is a difference of opinion? It might be the case that the only Christian traditions that come close to being deliberate about faith and power are the historic peace churches—Friends, Mennonite, and others. If your congregation is serious about power, think about what your children are learning about it.

Leadership Distilled

Discussing the topics in this chapter almost inevitably leads us into a consideration of the nature of leadership. What leadership is, what it looks like, what it takes to lead all are serious topics in the publishing and training worlds of recent years. In this book, we have suggested an image of leadership by proposing that pastoral ministry, power, and leadership overlap. They are not identical, although it is our hope that the practice of ministry would engage power in such a way that leadership occurs. It is tempting to draw this exploration of power and the church to a close by tossing out a simple, quotable definition for a phenomenon that is necessary for the vitality of Gospel witness. In our sound-bite world, such definitions are desired yet sometimes misleading. Leadership is more complex than all that, something that is easier to spot than it is to explain.

Rather than leaving readers with a single sound bite, I will offer you six. These points flow out of the lines of thought that the combined chapters have presented. Taken together, they provide you with an image of leadership that hopefully looks three-dimensional. Leadership is too important, and expects so much from those who seek it, to be treated in pat fashion. Think about these points separately, but also consider how they work together. Then you will be better prepared to engage power in your own ministry and see it result in leadership.

First, I am persuaded the more that I ruminate on this topic that leadership is really *more about leading*. Pay attention to the way in which the word "leader" is used in the media. It almost always refers to persons in an elected or appointed office. This implies that people in positions of authority are leading, simply by virtue of being in office. We hope that they are, but that is not always the case. Instead, I believe that the direction of this book proposes an understanding of leadership that is more fluid. We see leadership as leading—in incidents, episodes, opportunities, periods of change. It is not that leading takes place by happenstance in a fleeting moment, but neither does leading happen just because someone with bright ideas, energy, or connections gets elected to office. Leading does happen over some period of time in which a group or community faces some need and deals with it constructively. Whether the officers of the group or members of the community are leading in that experience depends upon what they are doing. Sometimes it is persons outside of formal structures who provide the impetus for what needs to be done.

This view suggests, secondly, that leadership is not a static thing; *it floats* within community, from person to person, and between groups. Since election or appointment cannot *make* leaders, actions and behaviors that end up leading a community can come from a variety of directions. Some of the dynamics of leadership emerge from the cultural confluence that is at play at the moment, as well as whether the group is facing a crisis. Few students of history would deny that Abraham Lincoln and Winston Churchill led their respective nations during a time of great testing. Yet the visible figures of history do not exhaust the list of those who have led. Leading can and does occur also behind the scenes, in places where the public eye is not so interested.

Third, leadership *requires learning*. Any person (pastor, minister, elected church officer) or group (church board) who aspires to lead must be willing and able to find out what they do not know. This requires not only the acquisition of raw information but also the ability to interpret it and process it through the person's or group's own cultural standpoint. Handling one's own fear and anxiety is also a prerequisite to lead. Both kinds of learning—factual and emotional/cultural—strengthen the capacity for leading.

Fourth, the potential for leadership is strengthened by *experiences with marginality*. People and groups who do lead have been influenced in significant ways with a prior (and perhaps even present) conscious awareness of not fitting into the world around them.[15] This was the case with persons who rescued Jews during World War II.[16] The point here is not that every person or group who lives in marginality becomes a leader. Rather, people who lead are able, for one thing, to draw upon their own confusing and frustrating experiences of being on the edge. That marginality might be based upon being a person of color, of having some form of cross-cultural experience, of being a girl who wanted to do "boy" things, or any other context that prompted feelings of being left out. There is no formulaic way of determining marginality. For those who want to make a difference in church or the world, meditating on one's own marginality can empower one's capacity to lead.

Fifth, leadership *shares power*. Eric Law has developed models of spirituality, leadership, change process, and power that offer Christians clear resources for learning how to lead. One of his claims is that Christians need to learn to share power between groups that are perceived to be in control and those that are not. This reiterates a point made in chapter 3. Law supports this very practical goal with theology; namely, that the Gospel hinges on death and resurrection. Groups that usually have power need to die to that power, giving it over to those groups in society that tend not to have power. Receiving power, for powerless communities, is like resurrection, like receiving new life. Yet the giving and receiving of power cannot end with one set of actions, Law argues. Those powerless who receive power then must share it with those from whom it was received. Within diverse communities (and they can be diverse in many ways), Law names this process "the cycle of Gospel living." Groups and persons learn to give and to receive power among themselves. The power of voice is one significant way to do this, a beginning point for sharing power in more systemic ways.[17] When those with access to power intentionally invite others to the table, they are leading. The pursuit of a more just and peaceful world, at whatever level one engages it, always creates leadership.[18]

Sixth and finally, leadership always *centers around vision.* Every group, every community, needs a compelling vision or it will flounder; hence, its energy will dissipate. For Christians, vision is a picture of their future with God, discerned in their midst. Keeping vision clear, articulate, and compelling is the ultimate challenge to leading. Any projects for bricks and mortar or program development must be interpreted clearly as fulfilling a vision that transcends the church's current situation. Otherwise, the church is just staying busy, and vision is fading.[19] If you care deeply about vision and want to put feet to it, you will be in a position to lead.

Power and Grace

Perhaps the final word about power that is appropriate for this book has to do with the Christian doctrine of grace. Where does all this talk about power take us? Is there any connection between power as it usually operates in the world and the apocalypse's vision of the new heaven and new earth (Rev. 21:1–5)? How can the actions of human beings, personally and collectively, ever contribute to God's purposes for creation? This line of questioning returns us to the methodological question from which we started. The way that things *are* (descriptively) and the way that things *should be* (theologically) meet in the same swamp. We must learn to maintain these two ways of looking at things with a tension that is creative, rather than separating the two and becoming either cynical (descriptive only) or idealistic (theological only). This book has sought to reclaim the side of this dynamic that is often viewed skeptically by many Christians and their churches.

It just might be the case that the clue rests in grace. At the heart of the entire biblical witness to God and the world, we discover again and again a vision of well-being that is initiated and carried out by God. We human beings, individually and collectively, can take no credit in coming up with the hope that the human race would be blessed (Genesis 8:20–9:17; 12:1–3; Isaiah 65:17–25). If we take the Bible seriously, we certainly must own the reality of humanity's proclivity for working at cross purposes with God. To be sure, key figures and communities have been at the center of God's purposes, and Christians claim to have inherited the mantle of responsibility for sharing this Good News. Such a weighty claim, however, is not one to wear with the kind of pride that would lord over others (Matthew 20:25). Such pride leads to forms of power, potentially abusive ones. How can we, especially as believers, over-come the desire for power that benefits some at the expense of others?

I think we are starting to get the hang of this swamp thing!

Perhaps grace can be our intersection between power and life. The lesson of the Tower of Babel seems in part to be that humans are tempted to take God's place. We seek to impose our own preferences as ultimate, caught in the small world of our particular group's view of life and the power that we want it to wield. When we treat ourselves and our ways as godlike, we are in danger of being deluded into maintaining our position at all costs. To one extent or another, all human communities face this temptation.[20] What happens, instead, to our sense of power-seeking when our personal lives and our human structures are built on grace? What does power look like as persons and groups confess their sins, receive forgiveness, and trust in the communion of the Holy Spirit at every turn?

As Eric Law argues, there is a rhythm in the life of faith that the community of faith is called to enter. It is a rhythm encircling both death and life, both the receiving and the release of power. Because of the deeper dimensions (i.e., the mud) of our American macroculture, perhaps a Christian way of engaging power still struggles to be heard. Alfred North Whitehead's observation that the Western world's "fashioning of God in the image of...imperial rulers" led him to comment that "the brief Galilean vision of humility flickered throughout the ages, uncertainly."[21] It is the hope of all the writers in this book that this vision will not be lost but sought anew. It is the prayer of those who have written here that our discussions of power will help to make this vision more fully present in this, the world that God made and keeps remaking.

Notes

Chapter 1

1. For a summary of European higher education, curriculum, and philosophy in the context of the development of medieval life, see Thomas H. Greer, *A Brief History of the Western World*, 5th ed. (San Diego: Harcourt Brace Jovanovich, 1987), chap. 6, esp. 219–27.

2. A helpful summary and critique of the development of modern science and its effects upon Western worldview and practice can be found in Alfred North Whitehead, *Science and the Modern World* (New York: The Free Press, 1925). Most to the point are chapters I, III, IV and V, and then chapter XII, "Religion and Science."

3. See "Welcome to the Family! Have You Been Adopted Yet?" chap. 2 in George B. Thompson, *How to Get Along with Your Church: Creating Cultural Capital for Doing Ministry* (Cleveland: The Pilgrim Press, 2001).

4. See, for example, Leas's early publication, *A Lay Person's Guide to Conflict Management* (Alban Institute, 1975).

5. Hugh Halverstadt's *Managing Church Conflict* (Louisville: Westminster/ John Knox Press, 1991), provides one of the more sustained and careful processes for handling church conflict. His model is somewhat complicated, however, and one can beg the question whether conflict resolution ever offers lasting benefits for the congregation.

6. John C. Harris, *Stress, Power and Ministry: An Approach to the Current Dilemmas of Pastors and Congregations*, rev. ed. (1977; Alban Institute, 1982), 7, 56.

7. Ibid., 20. See also p. 53: "Tension is not a negative state; it is the positive precondition of renewal and rebirth in all organized forms of life."

8. Ibid., 48.

9. "Effective Influence and the Fear of Powerlessness," chap. 6 in ibid.

10. Ibid. See, for instance, 19, 33, 55, and 118.

11. "Effective Influence," ibid., 44.

12. See ibid.: 'It is in this more personal and psychological sense that I want to use the concept of power—'the ability to affect, influence and change other persons.'" Rollo May, *Power and Innocence* (New York: W.W. Norton, 1972), 100.

13. Roy Oswald, *Power Analysis of a Congregation* (Alban Institute, 1981).

14. Ibid., 3.

15. Ibid., 4.

16. Ibid., 5–8.

17. Walter Wink, *Naming the Powers: The Language of Power in the New Testament*, vol. 1 of *The Powers Trilogy* (Philadelphia: Fortress Press, 1984), ix–x.

18. Ibid., 102.

19. Ibid., 104.

20. For a quick comparison of worldviews that Wink names and contrasts with his unraveling of New Testament powers, see Walter Wink, *Engaging the Powers: Discernment and Resistance in a World of Domination*, vol. 3 of *The Powers Trilogy* (Philadelphia: Fortress Press, 1992), 3–7.

21. Wink, *Naming the Powers*, 105, 107.

22. Ibid., n. 3.

23. Ibid., 110.

24. Carl S. Dudley and Earle Hilgert, *New Testament Tensions and the Contemporary Church* (Philadelphia: Fortress Press, 1987).

25. Social-scientific analysis in biblical exegesis has a history of its own. Two of the earliest publications in this field are Gerd Thiessen, *Sociology of Early Palestinian Christianity* (Philadelphia: Fortress Press, 1977), and Wayne Meeks, *The First Urban Christians* (New Haven: Yale University Press, 1983).

26. Greer, *Brief History of the Western World*, 118–24.

27. Ibid., 181–82.

28. Ibid., 185–87.

193

29. For a summary of the points in this paragraph, see Greer, 247–52.

30. John Kenneth Galbraith, "Power and Organization," in Steven Lukes, ed., *Power* (New York: New York University Press), 220ff.

31. For a discussion of the notion of freedom of association, see "The Indispensable Discipline of Social Responsibility," chap. 8 in James Luther Adams, *Voluntary Associations,* ed. J. Ronald Engel (Chicago: Exploration Press, 1986). For discussion on mediating structures, see "Mediating Structures and the Separation of Powers," chap. 12 in ibid.

32. The primary source for this section is Lukes.

33. Bertrand Russell, "The Forms of Power," in Lukes, 19, 25–27.

34. Max Weber, "Domination by Economic Power and by Authority," in Lukes, 28; Robert Dahl, "Power as the Control of Behavior," in Lukes, 40.

35. Weber, "Domination," 29.

36. See Galbraith, "Power and Organization," 212.

37. Weber, "Domination," 28–30, 33.

38. See Max Weber, "The Basic Categories of Social Organization," in *Weber: Selections in Translation,* ed. W. G. Runciman, trans. Eric Matthews (Cambridge: Cambridge University Press, 1978), 38.

39. Dahl, "Power as the Control of Behavior," 37, 55.

40. Talcott Parsons, "Power and the Social System," in Lukes, 137, 94.

41. Ibid., 101, 117.

42. See ibid., 130ff.

43 Michel Foucault, "Disciplinary Power and Subjection,' in Lukes, 233–34.

44. Nicos Poulantzas, "Class Power," in Lukes, 144–45.

Chapter 2

1. Walter Becker, "Self-Concept," in *Dictionary of Pastoral Care and Counseling,* ed. Rodney Hunter (Nashville: Abingdon Press, 1990), 1127.

2. Arthur Combs, *Being and Becoming* (New York: Springer Press, 1999), 34.

3. Combs continues this discussion throughout the chapter. This particular comment can be found in ibid., 47.

4. Robert Kegan, *The Evolving Self* (Cambridge: Harvard University Press, 1982), 42.

5. Carol Gilligan, *In A Different Voice: Psychological Theory and Women's Development* (Cambridge: Harvard University Press, 1982). Gilligan presents a documented study of the differences in development of girls and boys.

6. Riet Bons-Storm, *The Incredible Woman* (Nashville: Abingdon, 1966), 66–67.

7. Carol M. Miles, "And Your Daughters Shall Prophecy." *INSIGHTS* (Austin Seminary: Spring 2004): 9. This article has good insight into the perceptions of women in ministry. Dr. Miles is an associate professor in homiletics at Austin Theological Seminary.

8. Ibid., 10.

9. Young Lee Hertig, "Asian North American Women in the Workplace," in *People on the Way: Asian North Americans Discovering Christ, Culture, and Community,* ed. David Ng (Valley Forge: Judson Press, 1996), 107.

10. Ibid., 109.

11. For further discussion of the implications of the Transitions Group see Beverly Brigman, "Seeking God in the Midst of Transition" (D. Min. diss., Columbia Theological Seminary, 2000).

12. Teresa L. Fry Brown, "Avoiding Asphyxiation," *Embracing the Spirit,* ed. Emile M. Townes (Maryknoll: Orbis Books, 1997), 72.

13. Walter Wink, *Unmasking the Powers: The Invisible Forces That Determine Human Existence* (Philadelphia: Fortress Press, 1986), 78–82.

14. Rosita deAnn Mathews, "Using Power from the Periphery," *A Troubling In My Soul,* ed. Emile M. Townes (Maryknoll: Orbis Books, 1997), 98.

15. Ibid., 93. Mathews's discussion contains helpful reminders for those who feel that they live on the margins.

16. Ibid.

17. Ibid., 94–95.

18. Patricia Hunter, "And God Said: 'That's Good'," in *A Troubling In My Soul*, 191.

19. See, for instance, Eric H. F. Law, *Sacred Acts, Holy Change: Faithful Diversity and Practical Transformation* (St. Louis: Chalice Press, 2002).

20. Eric H. F. Law, *The Wolf Shall Dwell with the Lamb: A Spirituality for Leadership in a Multicultural Community* (St. Louis: Chalice Press, 1993), 17.

21. Ibid., 18–22.

22. George D. Parsons, *PACE Profile* (Eugene, Ore.: George D. Parsons, 1992).

23. Ibid., 7.

24. Ibid., 8.

25. Ibid., 9.

26. Ibid., 10.

27. Daniel Goleman, Richard Boysazis, and Annie McKee, *Primal Leadership: Learning to Lead with Emotional Intelligence* (Cambridge: Harvard Business School Press, 2002).

28. "The Neuroanatomy of Leadership," chap. 3 in ibid., esp. p. 39; see also Appendix B, that the skills can be acquired is claimed early on in the book: "These EI competencies are not innate talents but learned abilities" (p. 38).

Chapter 3

1. This definition comes from my earlier book, see *How to Get Along*, 6; see also the discussion of definitions of culture in my *Treasures in Clay Jars: New Ways to Understand Your Church* (Cleveland: The Pilgrim Press, 2003), 56.

2. The field of organizational culture has roots back to about 1970 and has received its most sustained theoretical and practical development since the 1980s. To my knowledge, the most significant author in the field is Edgar Schein, whose work will be referenced below.

3. For an introduction to understanding church conflict within a cultural framework, see "Handling Conflict: What If Things Go Sour?" chap. 6 in *How to Get Along*, esp. pp. 100–109.

4. See, for instance, Nancy Ammerman, et al., *Congregation and Community* (New Brunswick: Rutgers University Press, 1997), for a national study of 23 congregations that responded to contextual change in varying ways.

5. For more on the use of land mines as a metaphor of dangerous pastoral mistakes and how to avoid them, see "Land Mines: How Well Do You Know What You're Getting Into?" chap. 1 in *How to Get Along*.

6. Edgar Schein has written carefully and with great conceptual insight about managing group anxiety. See his *Organizational Culture and Leadership*, 2d ed. (San Francisco: Jossey-Bass, 1992), 22–23, 237–38, and his discussion of "the dynamics of change," 299–303.

7. See *How to Get Along*, sections in every chapter. Some of these same concepts are explained in the earlier *Futuring Your Church: Finding Your Vision and Making It Work* (Cleveland: United Church Press, 1999), esp. chap. 3. A more extended and overlapping discussion of anthropology appears in "Making Your Way Around the Village: Congregation as Bearer of Meaning," chap. 3 in *Treasures in Clay Jars*, 53–88.

8. Besides Schein, *Organizational Culture and Leadership*, chap. 2, "Uncovering the Levels of Culture," see also Eric Law, "Digging Down Deep to Facilitate Profound Change," in *Sacred Acts, Holy Change*, 33–45.

9. See Schein, 14–15, 255–56, 314–15

10. For a thorough outline of these deeper aspects of submerged culture, see Schein, "Assumptions About Reality, Truth, Time, and Space" (chap. 6) and "Assumptions About Human Nature, Activity, and Relationships" (chap. 7).

11. Edgar Schein has done extensive theoretical and methodological work on

organizational culture and how to discover its depths. On this matter of ease and precision in uncovering the submerged elements of an organization's culture, he says, "There is no reliable, quick way to identify cultural assumptions" (Schein, *Organizational Culture and Leadership,*194). For more insight on processes for ascertaining the submerged layer, see chap. 8, "Deciphering Culture for Insiders," and chap. 9, "Reporting About Culture to Outsiders."

12. For a brief discussion of status and its effect in congregations, see my *Treasures in Clay Jars,* 35–37.

13. Development of a thesis about regional power probably has remained so far the purview of political scientists. I contend, however, that cultural analysis of American regional subcultures would yield significant insights into differences between long-standing respective social and political processes. To my knowledge, such an analysis, using the concepts outlined in the present chapter, has not yet been undertaken.

14. For discussion of class as a sociological concept and its application to churches, see my brief presentation in *Treasures in Clay Jars,* 37–39.

15. The term "traditional orality" was coined by Tex Sample to encompass the concept being described in this section. Sample's account of this global and pervasive cultural phenomenon in its American forms and its relevance to pastoral ministry is concise and very readable. See Tex Sample, *Ministry in an Oral Culture: Living with Will Rogers, Uncle Remus and Minnie Pearl* (Louisville: Westminster/John Knox Press, 1994). The general ideas from this section of the present work draw upon Sample.

16. Effective strategies for engaging oral culture in parish ministry are suggested in my *How to Get Along,* 33–37.

17. The major published text on the subject of generational theory is William Strauss and Neil Howe, *Generations: The History of America's Future, 1584 to 2069*

(New York: William Morrow, 1991). An earlier version of generational theory, written for church audiences, is presented in Douglas Walrath, *Frameworks: Patterns for Living and Believing Today* (New York: The Pilgrim Press, 1987).

18. The earliest popular book on organizational culture was Terrence E. Deal and Allen A. Kennedy, *Corporate Cultures: The Rites and Rituals of Corporate Life* (Reading, Pa.: Addison-Wesley Publishing Co., 1982). The most comprehensive and useful lifecycle theory of organizations is found in Ichak Adizes, *Corporate Lifecycles: How and Why Organizations Grow and Die and What You Can Do About It* (Englewood Cliffs, N.J.: Prentice Hall, 1988). Versions appear in very general form in more recent religious publications. For instance, see Norman Shawchuck and Roger Heuser, "Understanding the Congregation's Life Cycle," chap. 11 in *Leading the Congregation: Caring for Yourself While Serving Others* (Nashville: Abingdon Press, 1993); see also Alice Mann, *Can Our Church Live? Redeveloping Congregations in Decline* (Alban Institute, 1999), 40ff.

19. For more information on these features, see Adizes, "Predicting the Quality of Decisions," chap. 5 in *Corporate Lifecycles.*

20. One of the "classics" here is H. Richard Niebuhr's *Christ and Culture* (New York: Harper & Brothers, 1951). The method in this book is theological, i.e., an examination of what several theologians have said about the relationship between the Gospel and the human world that the Gospel addresses. As I have tried to suggest, even up to this point in the chapter, is that Christians will be better both at analysis and strategy by bringing social scientific categories into the conversation on human experience.

21. Law, *Wolf Shall Dwell,* 17.

22. This is a phrase that Law uses frequently throughout the book; see ibid., 23.

23. Ibid., 17–18.

24. The introduction to this concept is found in "Differences in the Perception of Power and Their Consequences for Leadership," chap. 3 in ibid., 29–36.

25. Ibid., 18–22.

26. Law's strategy on sharing power indeed is based upon both anthropology and theology. It is too important to try to summarize in too brief of a space. See ibid., chap. 6, "Who Has Power and Who Doesn't?" 53–62, and chap. 7, "Living Out the Fullness of the Gospel in the Peaceable Realm," 71–78.

27. Both quotations in this paragraph come from Law, *Wolf Shall Dwell*, 27.

28. See "Mutual Invitation as Mutual Empowerment," chap. 9 in ibid., 79–88.

29. For instance, Law also promotes "form-centered" rather than "person-centered" liturgy, which he argues is another significant way to share power. See "Liturgy as Spiritual Discipline for Leadership in a Multicultural Community," chap. 11 in ibid., 99–112.

30. Ibid., 13.

31. See *How to Get Along*, 1–26, 27–44.

32. Alfred North Whitehead, *Adventures of Ideas* (New York: The Free Press, 1933), 274.

Chapter 4

1. Clarence N. Stone, *Regime Politics: Governing Atlanta, 1946–1988* (Lawrence: University Press of Kansas, 1989), 6.

2. Floyd Hunter, *Community Power Structure: A Study of Decision Makers* (Chapel Hill: University of North Carolina Press, 1953).

3. Paul E. Peterson, *City Limits* (Chicago: University of Chicago Press, 1981).

4. Dennis R. Judd and Susan S. Fainstein, eds., *The Tourist City* (New Haven: Yale University Press, 1999).

5. Bernard J. Frieden and Lynne B. Sagalyn, *Downtown Inc.: How America Rebuilds Cities* (Cambridge, Mass.: MIT Press, 1989), and Harvey K. Newman,

Southern Hospitality: Tourism and the Growth of Atlanta (Tuscaloosa and London: University of Alabama Press, 1999).

6. Harvey K. Newman, "Decentralization of Atlanta's Convention Business,"*Urban Affairs Review* 38, no. 2 (November 2002): 249.

7. Hunter, *Community Power Structure.*

8. Newman, *Southern Hospitality.*

9. Robert A. Dahl, *Who Governs?* (New Haven: Yale University Press, 1961).

10. Stone, R*egime Politics*, 8–9.

11. Ibid.,184.

12. John R. Logan and Harvey L. Molotch, *Urban Fortunes: The Political Economy of Place* (Berkeley: University of California Press, 1987).

13. Ibid.

14. Ibid., 78.

15. Harvey K. Newman, "God and the Growth Machine," *Review of Religious Research* 32, no. 3 (March 1991): 241.

16. Stone, *Regime Politics*, 192.

17. Ibid., 192–94.

18. Ibid., 110.

19. Robert A. Beauregard, *Voices of Decline: The Postwar Fate of U.S. Cities* (Cambridge: Blackwell, 1993).

20. Michel Foucault, "The Subject and Power," in *Beyond Structuralism and Hermeneutics,* ed. H. L. Dreyfus and P. Rabinow (Chicago: University of Chicago Press, 1982), 208–26.

21. Stone, *Regime Politics,* 212.

22. Harvey K. Newman, "Historic Preservation Policy and Regime Politics in Atlanta," *Journal of Urban Affairs* 23, no. 1 (2001): 71–86.

23. Barbara E. Phillips, *City Lights: Urban-Suburban Life in the Global Society* (New York: Oxford University Press, 1996), 388.

24. Chester Hartman, *Yerba Buena: Land Grab and Community Resistance in San Francisco* (San Francisco: Glide Press, 1973).

25. Andre Bieler, *The Social Humanism of Calvin* (Richmond: John Knox Press, 1964), 25.

26. Ibid.

27. W. Fred Graham, *The Constructive Revolutionary: John Calvin and his Socio-Economic Impact* (Atlanta: John Knox Press, 1978), 62.

28. Stone, *Regime Politics*.

Chapter 5

1 Richard G. Watts, *The Good Samaritan: Presbyterians and Public Policy* (Louisville: Presbyterian Peacemaking Program, 1988)

2. Jim Watkins, *Living Faithfully in the Public Square* (Louisville: Presbyterian Peacemaking Program, 1999), 12, 13.

3. John T. McNeill, ed. *Calvin: Institutes of the Christian Religion IV*, trans. Ford Lewis Battles (Philadelphia: Westminster Press, 1960) Bk. IV, ch. XX, 4.

4. Watkins, *Living Faithfully*, 7.

5. *Institutes of the Christian Religion*, Bk. IV, ch. XX, 8.

6. Watkins, *Living Faithfully*, 15, 16.

7. John Glenn, as quoted in Kimberly Richter, Jim Watkins, and Vera White, *Rebuilding: Peacemaking in Nehemiah* (Louisville, Ky.: Presbyterian Peacemaking Program, 1996), 5.

8. Walter Brueggeman, *To Act Justly, Love Tenderly, Walk Humbly* (Mahwah, N.J.: Paulist Press, 1986), 5.

9. A portion of the commentary is based on material located in "Politics and the New Testament" by Sara Winter, "The Living Pulpit" (April/June 1996).

10. "Christian Obedience in a Nuclear Age," PCUSA General Assembly Minutes, 450.

11. More suggestions on communicating with public officials can be found in Jim Watkins, *Making a Difference in the Public Arena* (Louisville: Presbyterian Peacemaking Program, 1993).

12. For more information on seeking public office, see Jim Watkins, *Double Knot Your Shoelaces: A Guide for Running Grassroots Campaigns* (Louisville: Presbyterian Peacemaking Program, 1996).

13. From the Opening Devotional of the Georgia House of Representatives, Feb. 4, 1994.

Chapter 6

1. John Harris, *Stress, Power and Ministry: An Approach to the Current Dilemmas of Pastors and Congregations* (Alban Institute, 1977), 69–71.

2. For more information on how persons tend to behave under "bad" stress, see George Parsons, *PACE Profile*, esp. 7–10, under the "Dis-stress" columns of each page.

3. A very insightful summary of the relationship between managing anxiety and leading is found in Edgar Schein, *Organizational Culture and Leadership*, 298–301, 386–92.

4. "Self-awareness' and 'self-management" are terms from Goleman's, Boyatzis's, and McKee's work; see Goleman, Boyatzis, and McKee, *Primal Leadership*, 39.

5. See "Land Mines," in *How to Get Along*, 22–23.

6. The modern classic on the subject of leadership is Robert K. Greenleaf, *Servant Leadership: A Journey into the Nature of Legitimate Power and Greatness* (New York: Paulist Press, 1977). Other notable titles include John W. Gardner, *On Leadership* (New York: The Free Press, 1990); Stephen R. Covey, *Principle-Centered Leadership* (New York: Simon & Schuster, 1990); Edgar Schein, *Organizational Culture and Leadership*; Margaret J. Wheatley, *Leadership and the New Science: Learning about Organization from an Orderly Universe* (San Francisco: Berrett-Koehler, 1992); Ronald A. Heifetz, *Leadership without Easy Answers* (Cambridge: The Belknap Press, 1994); and John P. Kotter, *Leading Change* (Boston:

Harvard Business School Press, 1996).

7. Lovett H. Weems, Jr., "Vision," chap. 2 in *Church Leadership: Vision, Team, Culture, Integrity* (Nashville: Abingdon Press, 1993).

8. Ibid. See also "Ahead of the Troops," chap. 5 in *How to Get Along.*

9. For a concise, nontechnical discussion of American religious disestablishment, see Paul Johnson, *A History of the American People* (New York: Harper Collins, 1997), 204–11, esp. 209. See also similar comment in Winthrop S. Hudson and John Corrigan, *Religion in America: An Historical Account of the Development of American Religious Life,* 5th ed. (New York: Macmillan, 1992), 104–5.

10. For an explanation of the concept of cultural capital and how it functions in congregations, see my *How to Get Along,* 21–24, 49–52, 59–60, 67–71, 112, 127–30.

11. See Edgar Schein's discussion on this matter in "How to Study and Interpret Culture," part 3 in *Organizational Culture and Leadership.* Since his context is business organizations, some of the steps in his model need to be modified for use in church. I have done some of this kind of modification in *How to Get Along,* esp. 53–56, 97–103 and chap. 4 ("Effective Delivery").

12. See, for instance, Leonard Sweet, *Soul Tsunami: Sink or Swim in New Millennium Culture* (Grand Rapids: Zondervan, 1999).

13. Stories of twenty-three congregations dealing with change in their communities are told in Nancy Ammerman et al., *Congregation and Community* (New Brunswick: Rutgers University Press, 1997).

14. See Schein on unfreezing and refreezing, 298–305; see also John Kotter, *Leading Change,* 143–58.

15. See Schein, *Organizational Culture and Leadership,* 386–87, for his comments about the value of "boundary-spanning perception."

16. See Douglas K. Huneke, *The Moses of Rovno* (New York: Dodd, Mead and Company, 1985), 179–80, for a summary of the "social marginality" of Fritz Graebe, who rescued hundreds of Jews during World War II.

17. Law's summary of this cycle is found in *Wolf Shall Dwell,* 73–75.

18. Law's process of "mutual invitation" is one of the most useful ways for developing a dynamic of sharing power in small groups and meetings. See "Mutual Invitation as Mutual Empowerment," chap. 9 in ibid.

19. For a helpful listing of characteristics and functions of vision, see Lovett Weems, "Vision," chap. 2 in *Church Leadership.*

20. See Eric Law's interpretation of the Tower of Babel narrative in "Up and Down the Tower of Babel," chap. 6 in *The Bush Was Blazing.*

21. Alfred North Whitehead, *Process and Reality,* corrected ed., ed. David Ray Griffin and Donald W. Sherburne (New York: The Free Press, 1978), 342.

Other books from The Pilgrim Press

Treasures in Clay Jars
New Ways to Understand Your Church
George B. Thompson, Jr.
Foreword by James Fowler
ISBN 0-8298-1566-X/paper/224 pages/$21.00

This resource is designed to provide persons in training for ministry with a paradigm-shifting framework to interpret and work effectively with the complex dynamics of local faith communities. Thompson utilizes explicit and relevant conceptual and theoretical tools from fields such as sociology, economics, and cultural anthropology to engage those who will become pastors to work effectively with 21st-century congregations.

How To Get Along with Your Church
Creating Cultural Capital for Ministry
George B. Thompson Jr.
ISBN 0-8298-1437-X/paper/176 pages/$17.00

This resource incorporates Thompson's research and observations on pastoring a church. He finds that the pastors who are most successful in engaging their parishioners are the ones who develop "cultural capital" within their congregations, meaning that they invest themselves deeply into how their church does its work and ministries.

Futuring Your Church
Finding Your Vision and Making It Work
George B. Thompson, Jr.
ISBN 0-8298-1331-4/paper/128 pages/$14.95

This resource allows church leaders to explore their congregation's heritage, its current context, and its theological bearings. Dr. Thompson provides insights that enable church members to discern what God is currently calling the church to do in this time and place. It is a practical, helpful tool for futuring ministry.

The Generation Driven Church
Evangelizing Boomers, Busters and Millennials
William and Le Etta Benke
ISBN 0-8298-1509-0/paper/128 pages/$13.00

The Benkes seek to revitalize the ministries of small and midsize churches by helping them to adjust to the changing culture. It also offers strategic approaches that will re-orient ministries to attract younger generations and take churches with an "inward focus" (churches devoid of conversion growth because of the absence of meaningful outreach to un-churched adults who comprise the post-modernist cultures) to an "outreach focus."

Behold I Do a New Thing
Transforming Communities of Faith
C. Kirk Hadaway
ISBN 0-8298-1430-2/paper/160 pages/$15.00

Recent talk and thinking about congregations concentrate on declining church attendance. Author Kirk Hadaway thinks an important part of the conversation is missing—how can churches, in spite of the decline, remain engaged in the mission of transforming lives? Looking at churches in new ways and holding new expectations will allow church leadership to guide congregations in the journey where transformation and renewal is constant and embraced.

The Big Small Church Book
David R. Ray
ISBN 0-8298-0936-8/paper/256 pages/$15.95

Over sixty percent of churches have fewer than seventy-five people in attendance each Sunday. The Big Small Church Book contains information on everything from practical business matters to spiritual development. Clergy and lay leaders of big churches can learn much here as well.

Legal Guide for Day-to-Day Church Matters
A Hand Book for Pastors and Church Leaders—Revised and Expanded
Cynthia S. Mazur and Ronald K. Bullis
ISBN 0-8298-0990-2/paper/148 pages/$10.00

This book belongs on every pastor's desk because the church is not exempt from the growing number of lawsuits filed each year. The authors are clergy as well as attorneys.

To order these or any other books from The Pilgrim Press call or write to:
The Pilgrim Press
700 Prospect Avenue East
Cleveland, Ohio 44115-1100

Phone orders: 1-800-537-3394 • Fax orders: 216-736-2206
Please include shipping charges of $4.00 for the first book and $0.75 for each additional book.

Or order from our web sites at *www.pilgrimpress.com* and *www.ucpress.com*.

Prices subject to change without notice.